Black Saturday

HMS Royal Oak.

FORTUNES OF WAR

Black Saturday:
Tragedy at Scapa Flow

ALEXANDER MCKEE

CERBERUS

First published in the UK, by Souvenir Press, Horwitz Edition, 1959.

PUBLISHED IN THE UNITED KINGDOM BY;
Cerberus Publishing Limited
22A Osprey Court
Hawkfield Business Park
Bristol
BS14 0BB
UK
e-mail: cerberusbooks@aol.com
www.cerberus-publishing.com

British Library Cataloguing in Publication Data.
A catalogue record for this book is available from the British Library.

ISBN 1 84145 045 6

PRINTED AND BOUND IN ENGLAND.

Contents

Dedication

Only one decoration was ever awarded in connection with the sinking of HMS *Royal Oak*; it went to Skipper Gatt of the drifter *Daisy II*, and no man more deserved it. Because there were no officers present in the messdecks, to testify to what happened there, a number of other men – some of whom are dead – did not, and could not, achieve any recognition for their actions. This book, based on the testimony of their shipmates, may perhaps go a little way towards remedying that. 'Fearful lights that never beckon, save when kings and heroes die,' wrote Aytoun of the Northern Lights which were said to have nickered earlier that night above Scapa Flow. Not all the men whose actions are recounted here were heroes; but some of them were.

Foreword

My earliest memento of HMS *Royal Oak* is a Christmas card received from her when she was on neutrality patrol off the north coast of Spain during the Civil War; the sender was killed later at Dunkirk. My next connection with the ship was when I met a survivor about ten days after the sinking; he told his story extremely well, and I often wish I could have recorded it. Subsequently, I cut out and kept every reference to the event which I could find. Almost precisely nineteen years afterwards, I set out to reconstruct the drama of that night in Scapa Flow. My reason was that, although descriptions without number had been published, they were virtually all repetitions of Prien's story; there was little from the British side. In the end, I found that I had some sixty witnesses, whose accounts contradicted the previously published stories at almost every point.

I have read, I believe, most of what has been written about the *Royal Oak* and have drawn upon it, here and there, where it seemed reliable; but those occasions were regrettably rare. It would however be astonishingly reckless to claim that absolute accuracy has been achieved throughout, in reconstructing a bewilderingly swift succession of events which ended in death for two-thirds of the participants. I have not been able to question every witness to every brief scene; if I had, the descriptions might be modified slightly. Memory is selective. In particular, identifications of one man by another, unless he knew him well, cannot in these circumstances be regarded as absolutely certain.

Except in the few cases where it is expressly stated that a description is second-hand, it is based on one or more direct eye-witness accounts, some of them written down very shortly after the sinking. To preserve the authentic atmosphere I have used an equivalent to the best radio documentary technique of modelling the descriptions very closely on the originals, even where they are not directly quoted. Much of the narrative, where it concerns direct action, is therefore not a history at all; it is the nearest possible approach to the real thing, an account of the sinking by the men who were there, with the writer's role reduced to little more than that of selection, arranging and cutting.

I have, however, taken advantage of the fact that I was soon in possession of a mass of material not available to individual survivors, to bring some pattern into what, for those concerned, was often fragmentary and confusing. For these judgments the sole responsibility is mine. That is also true of the analysis of the log of U-47, although each point was intensively discussed with the survivors and a few outside, but expert, witnesses.

Alexander McKee
Rowlands Castle, February, 1959.

CHAPTER ONE

DEATH AT THE END OF THE WORLD

The Romans called the northern islands Ultima Thulae – the end of the world. As a matter of geography it was not true, but as an expression of what it feels like to be there as a southern stranger, it was, and is, exactly right.

When the Vikings landed on Orkney they felt sufficiently at home to settle there; it was so like the wild and savage coast from which they had sailed. Black, grained sheets of rock rose hundreds of feet out of the bursting Atlantic; cut into the cliffs by the pounding tides were great fiords, known as geos, each one a white, whirling cauldron of screaming seabirds. Only a few withered trees, like hunchbacked dwarfs, clung to the earth in the rare places free of the pouring wind, and picked skulls and bones of cattle lay in the heather. Half the time, the hills had their streaked backs in the clouds and grey vapour trailed over the black tarns, still and reptilian, which pocked their summits; there were valleys white with nesting gulls, which rose like a cloud on human approach, their thousand voices sounding like women lamenting 'Oh, oh, oh!' When the sun cut through, then the sea was revealed as an incredible waste of water that stretched to an infinite horizon – desolation without end. As it was then, so it is now.

To the town-bred sentries of the second world war, condemned to guard this wilderness for how many years they knew not, against an enemy who would never come, the monotony eventually brought a curious sickness not unlike the 'cafard.' The train bringing them back to the north, from leave, became the saddest train in the world; the south-bound train, the happiest. The stretch of water, in the centre of the circling islands, which they guarded, was eventually to become, as it had been in the first world war, the impregnable main anchorage of the British and Allied navies in European waters. But, in this sixth week of the second world war, its defences consisted largely of what little had not been removed, or rotted away, during twenty years of peace and disarmament. In name only, was it still 'Impregnable Scapa.'

It was precisely because of the undefended state of the anchorage that, on the night of 13th/14th October, 1939, it was almost deserted; all the important units of the Home Fleet had gone, in the apparently endless process of being rotated from one insecure base to another, in the hope of evading attack. And it was because the main threat was considered to be from the air, that the 19,000 ton battleship *Royal Oak* was anchored in the distant north-east corner of the Flow, to which her AA guns could give protection, instead of being in the south-west corner, near the naval base of Lyness, which was guarded by the only eight heavy AA guns then at Scapa.

At midnight precisely the watches in the ship changed over, but Sergeant J McLaverty of the Royal Marines continued to walk the forecastle for some minutes more, talking to Colour-Sergeant Harold C Paice, the senior NCO of the Marine detachment. Like most of the crew, both men were some 700 miles from home, which is nearly as far as you can get and still stay in the British Isles; both lived in Southsea, not far from the Marine barracks at Eastney. Southsea now would be blacked out, but curiously enough they had never seen a blackout in a city; the thing was so new that it had replaced the weather as topic of conversation and material for comedians throughout the country. It was, indeed, the only sign of war.

Of course, Scapa was blacked out, but it made hardly any difference to the ring of barren, sparsely populated islands; the Flow was not like Portsmouth harbour, with a city on two sides of it. It was enormous, and almost deserted. The actual naval base, Lyness – which was largely a collection of huts and some oil tanks – was ten miles away and hidden behind hills; Kirkwall, the small town which was the capital of Orkney, lay four miles away beyond the bow. There would be a few drifters in that direction, tied up to Scapa Pier. Two miles away to port the old seaplane carrier *Pegasus* was anchored, the only other ship at all in that part of the Flow. There was no sign of her, because she, too, was blacked out. Blackout regulations for the Home Fleet, laid down by the Commander-in-Chief, Admiral Forbes, consisted of painting the riding lights blue, so that they were visible only from a distance of two or three hundred yards, and the fitting of 'light-excluding ventilators' to the portholes instead of the glass-scuttles. These ventilators allowed air into the cabins and messdecks, while preventing the escape of any light; they were not, however, waterproof. If they were to be submerged, the sea would pour through in a torrent.

Paice and McLaverty could dimly make out the nearest pan of the mainland, which was half a mile away on the starboard beam, because the dark mass of the cliffs made a vague silhouette against the starlit night sky; but there was no moon, and the battleship herself was invisible from the Flow at anything over 250 yards. On nights like this her picket boat, returning late with the mail, had to steer a compass course towards her until the cox could see the radio masts on the hill behind her; knowing from there roughly where she lay, he would then alter course until, with luck, about 200 yards distant from the battleship, her riding lights became visible. The night was calm and cold; the tide, running fast along the sides of the *Royal Oak*, was now going out, for it was more than two hours after high tide; the temperature of that black water on this winter night was 48°F., cold enough to shock and numb a man within minutes.

The *Royal Oak* had virtually no life-saving equipment left; most of the Carley rafts had been smashed in a gale and the broken pieces were piled up on the forecastle, where Paice and McLaverty were walking; in an emergency, however, these would be better than nothing, and that was why they were there. McLaverty himself was the proud possessor of one of the few lifejackets in the ship. He was proud of it because it was German, given to him by a prisoner from a Dornier flying boat which had been shot down while shadowing the fleet. It gave him a pleasant feeling of actually being in the war. But there had been no general issue of lifejackets yet and the crew of the battleship were without any personal means of flotation in the water. That did not worry them at the moment, because they were safely in harbour behind defences which, so far as they knew, had proved unpenetrable for the whole five years of the first world war. Anyway, to those who live in her, a battleship – even an old one – always seems far too large, solid and comfortable to sink.

The *Royal Oak was* rather old. Indeed, that was why she had been left in Scapa; she was now too slow to keep up with the rest of the fleet. Her value was reduced to that of a floating AA battery in harbour or as 'long stop' in a complicated manoeuvre for heading off German warships, which was the role from which she had just returned; and no doubt she would have been useful for convoy work or coastal bombardment. She was one of the five ships of the *Royal Sovereign* class laid down under the 1913-14 estimates as cheap, coal-burning copies of the *Queen Elizabeths*. The *Royal Oak* was built at Devonport between January, 1914, and May, 1916, at a cost of just under two-and-a-half million pounds. In appearance, like her sister ships, she closely resembled the earlier *Queen Elizabeth* class which, however, had two funnels (later trunked into one). The general layout was exactly the same.

Amidships, the hull was built around four Parsons turbines and eighteen Yarrow oil-fired boilers, the change from coal to oil having been made while she was still under construction. This vital pan of the ship was shielded by what amounted to a gigantic, upturned tray of armour plate which was, in places, thirteen inches thick; it served to protect her propelling machinery from projectiles striking her deck and sides. It did not, and could not, extend very far below the waterline. The doors and hatches in this armoured belt were, naturally, kept to a minimum and were themselves so heavy that they could be opened only by machinery.

At either end of the propelling machinery amidships was dispersed the main punch of the battleship, the reason for her existence: eight fifteen-inch guns in four turrets, two just forward of the engines, two just aft of the boilers. The guns were protected by armour which in places was thirteen inches thick. The turrets revolved on barbettes, again thickly armoured, which went down several decks to the armoured belt, so that the shells and cordite charges coming up through them from the shell rooms and magazines below the waterline would be shielded during the dangerous passage to the guns.

The shell room for each turret held 208 fifteen-inch shells, the magazine next to it contained the appropriate number of cordite propellant charges; from above, these were protected by the armoured deck, capped by the barbettes and turrets. If a single enemy shell or bomb broke through a weak point to explode the cordite in a magazine, the shell room would explode within seconds, probably setting off the next shell room as well. The result would be a double bang, a cloud of smoke half-a-mile high, and about three survivors. It could happen accidentally, if the temperature of the cordite was allowed to rise; a ship could blow up at anchor, with no enemy near. To avoid a cordite explosion a system of safety vents was fitted which would allow the burning cordite to escape through the ship to the air, before it built up enough pressure to explode. The result would be a trail of havoc, of cindered corpses and terribly burnt men screaming in agony, but the ship would still be afloat and fighting.

Below the waterline the *Royal Oak* had no heavy armour protection for these vulnerable parts; there is a practical limit to the amount of armour that can be put in a ship, and a totally protected battleship would not float. Underwater protection was by the lighter means of anti-torpedo bulges, or 'blisters,' added as an afterthought to the original design. The result looked as if someone had sliced a gigantic sausage down the centre and stuck one half to the battleship's starboard side and the other half to her port side. A torpedo was supposed to spend its force on rending open the blister, leaving the hull intact or, at any rate, not very much damaged.

The actual bottom of the ship was the most vulnerable part; and the Germans had in fact a not-very-reliable magnetic fuse for a torpedo which would explode the warhead directly under the hull; for technical reasons, this was not likely to be used in the shallow waters of an anchorage but, when employed in the open sea, immensely increased the effect of a torpedo.

The hull was, of course, divided into a great many water-tight compartments but, as the ship was in harbour, not all the water-tight doors were closed. On most decks the alternate doors, on opposite sides of the ship, were open, so that it was not possible to walk inside the *Royal Oak* in a straight line from bow to stern; it was necessary continually to cross over from port to starboard and then back again. This gave a measure of protection against the flash from any sudden explosion and at the same time allowed work to go on normally. But if the ship were to be holed unexpectedly and without warning, the flooding could only be localised by closing the remaining water-tight doors – and that could only be done if there was power to operate the machinery or time enough for men to do the work manually.

In addition, the aims of the Gunnery branch, concerned exclusively with the problems of hitting other people, clashed frequently with the demands of Damage Control, responsible for the safety of their own ship, when hit. The latter might maintain that a particular opening should be closed, for protective purposes, while the former would insist that it be kept open, for ammunition supply. Gunnery was in the ascendant then, and gunnery almost always won.

At about thirty minutes after midnight, Colour-Sergeant Paice turned to McLaverty, and said he was going to turn in. McLaverty, however, walked up and down for a few more minutes. He did not normally stay up so late, but tonight he was First Duty and there had been one or two cases of overstayed leave, as well as men who had missed the boat for their own ships ten miles away at Lyness and had decided to put up for the night in the *Royal Oak*. One of them was a Chief Steward from the *Iron Duke*. Also, two men had been put into cells a few hours previously; they were directly below McLaverty, as he walked the forecastle.

Most of the crew, dead tired, had turned in early, glad to be back in the security of Scapa, where they could relax; to them the *Royal Oak* was something permanent, unshakable, unsinkable. McLaverty, who had joined the Navy in 1912, knew this was illusion. He had served before at Scapa, in the battleship *King George V*, and could remember still a night in July, 1917, when the woof-woof of a giant explosion rocked the anchorage and the whole Grand Fleet went to action stations, switching on their searchlights as if on a command. They swept across the water and settled on a spot where the battleship *Vanguard* had been; now, there was nothing, not even a ripple, merely a great cloud of smoke. McLaverty had been in one of the boats which had pulled away from the *King George V* to look for survivors, but they found on the water only a slimy coat of blood and oil. Other boats picked up a few men, he thought there had been three in all – and the ship's cat. A complete gun turret had been found on the island of Flotta, blown an incredible distance right out of the ship; and there were some pitiful bits and pieces, including a Marine's kitbag.

What really happened that night could never be known, but the verdict had been, 'lost by internal explosion.' It had been impossible to say whether the cause had been an accident in a magazine, leading to the explosion of a shell room, or if the disaster had a more sinister implication. An accident in a magazine always is a possibility, but there had been already a number of British warships – far too many – destroyed in harbour by unexplained internal explosions, the *Bulwark* at Sheerness and the *Natal* at Invergordon were probably the best known. There had been whispers of 'sabotage,' hard to prove or disprove. There had been similar talk about the loss of the cruiser *Hampshire* which, with Lord Kitchener aboard, had blown up on what was thought to be a mine off Marwick Head, in June, 1916, shortly after leaving Scapa for Russia.

When McLaverty went below to turn in, in the early hours of Saturday, 14th October, 1939, he was within half-an-hour of another Scapa Flow mystery; but this time he was to be an actual participant instead of a horrified spectator.

CHAPTER TWO

WAR STATIONS

The *Royal Oak* was a smart ship – possibly the smartest in the Navy. She commissioned in style on 7th June 1939. her crew marching out of RN Barracks, Portsmouth, behind a band, wheeling to the right, down Queen Street onto the Hard, and in through the Dockyard main gates to where the battleship lay alongside the Southern Railway Jetty. Her new commanding officer was Captain W H Benn, who had for his senior executive officer Commander R F Nichols. Lieutenant-Commander M F B Ward was First Lieutenant and Torpedo Officer, Lieutenant. Commander S D Roper was Gunnery Officer, Lieutenant-Commander R A V Gregory was the Navigator. Lieutenant-Commander F N Cook was from the Royal Australian Navy. One of the Lieutenants, 'Pony' Moore was an experienced submariner, doing his big ship time.

Most of the crew were local men from 'Pompey' though some came from Devonport, where the ship had been built, and a few were from the north-east coast. Not all were strangers to each other; a number of them had just paid off the *Courageous*, and so were shipmates already. It takes a little time for over 1,200 men to get to know each other, and shake down together into a team in a new ship; they were somewhat short of that point when the end came.

But on 7th June no one had any idea that they had a rendezvous to keep among the bleak northern isles. The *Royal Oak* was destined for two-and-a-half years in the Mediterranean. She sailed first on a shakedown cruise to Torquay and Portland, but events overtook her there. Hitler had already marched into Czechoslovakia, which was a strategic move on his part, to outflank Poland; for the first time he incorporated in the Reich a country which was not German. He began, as expected, to press for the return of the German part of Poland.

The Home Fleet sailed into Weymouth for a review – which can also be a polite method of mobilisation – but the ships afterwards dispersed to their home ports to give summer leave. Two weeks later the *Royal Oak* sailed for the last time from 'Pompey,' to take part in a Home Fleet convoy exercise. By the end of August the ships were concentrating at Scapa under war orders, though war had not yet broken out. The Communications ship *Greenwich* was first in, followed by the *Royal Oak*. They watched the *Iron Duke* – popularly known as the 'Iron Duck' – come in. She was Jellicoe's old flagship at Jutland, now partly demilitarised, and serving as a training and depot ship. The Duke of Wellington was nicknamed after the first ship to bear this name, which was, literally, the first HMS *Duke* to be built of iron. When a hospital ship, the *Saint Abba*, also sailed into the anchorage, glittering with white paint and red crosses, there was a roar of joking: 'Now we know there's going to be war – the Admiralty are taking care of everything.' In spite of all the indications most of them found it hard to believe that another world war was upon them. There had been a similar 'flap' the previous year.

Actual signs of warlike preparations, at Scapa, other than the gathering fleet, were few and far between. There were three main, easily navigable entrances to the eight-miles-square stretch of water which is Scapa Flow – the Sounds of Hoxa, Hoy and Switha. Each was guarded by a single line of nets which looked rather like a row of lobster pots – these were the 'flotations' which supported the two-inch wire net. In the centre of each line of nets was a 'gate,' which was merely a length of floating net which could be moved like a door, by two bar boats stationed on opposite sides of it, to let ships in or out. Daring submarine commanders who try to sneak through in the wake of a ship are usually dead submarine commanders in short order, because the trick is known. Small patrol vessels zig-zag in the entrance as soon as the 'gate' is opened, and as the ship passes through close up about her stern, watching for any signs of a submarine. These defences, however, were not as strong as they had been in the first world war, or as they would be again. It is perfectly possible for a submarine fitted with explosive wire-cutters to go through a single line of nets; it takes at least two lines of nets to first slow, and then stop, her. A really impregnable floating defence consists of an 'indicator' net (a sort of burglar alarm), or alternatively a controlled minefield, well forward of the main boom which should itself consist of four lines of nets. But most of this equipment had been removed after the first world war and had not yet been replaced; a bold and lucky submarine commander probably could have got through the booms at this stage of the war.

There were four other entrances to the Flow, all of them on the eastern side, all close together, all narrow, and only one of them navigable. This latter was Kirk Sound, which is part of Holm Sound, where it divides round the island of Lamb Holm. The channels on both sides of this island had been obstructed by the sinking in them, during the first world war, of blockships filled with concrete. Those blockships were still there. They were not, however, covered by fire – there were no coastal batteries in position. There was a village – St Mary's, or Holm – on the mainland side of Kirk Sound and a submarine coming past the blockships would have to pass this. This particular channel was, as it happens, not only navigable, but in use by ships of up to 600 tons. The blockships had been sunk, not bow to stern, but parallel and overlapping, so that there was a zig-zag gap – although from seaward, to the U-boat's-eye view, they would present the appearance of an absolutely continuous line of defence. That may have been deliberate, but in a new war in which air photography would undoubtedly reach out to Scapa, it was an omission which ought to have been repaired. In fact, plans were on foot to do this and a suitable additional blockship had already been earmarked by the Admiralty. However, it was soon to be sunk on its way north.

Local skippers considered it impossible to get through that channel except at certain conditions of the tide. It was not that there was not enough water, but that the water went through too fast. The Pentland Firth outside compresses the full power of the Atlantic between rocky walls, making it probably the worst stretch of water around the British Isles; this tide forces its way through Holm Sound with furious energy. To come in with the tide is – or rather, was, because 'the channel has now been blocked by a causeway – rather like riding a canoe down a Rocky Mountain river; The only practical method, in their view, was to make the passage against the tide, thus slowing and steadying the vessel. This was particularly applicable to a submarine, which, because it has very little buoyancy, tends to make a pig-like sort of wallow instead of a turn. It is easy enough for a submarine to go out of harbour sideways, if the current is right.

Very shortly after the *Royal Oak* arrived at Scapa, 'Pony' Moore, who was divisional officer of the 120 Boys she carried, decided to make his own survey of the defences. He had a look at Kirk Sound and came back to tell his friends that he, personally, would have no hesitation at all in bringing in a small submarine through that channel. And he forthwith made an official report to that effect. Nobody took very much notice, because it was thought he was inclined to exaggerate.

Anyway, the submarine was believed to be under control, because of Asdic, a piece of detection apparatus of which the Navy was very proud; a very much greater threat was believed to lie in the air, at any rate to warships lying at anchor in an under-defended base. According to information in the possession of the Admiralty, the *Luftwaffe* was capable of launching an 800-bomber attack on Scapa Flow – which meant 100 bombers to every heavy AA gun there. This alarming news was sent to Admiral Forbes on 7th September. There was a tendency throughout the first few years of the war grossly to exaggerate the strength of the *Luftwaffe*, possibly a legacy from Mr Churchill's '20,000 first-line German aircraft' which had caused much merriment in the aeronautical press just before the war. One editor who had been particularly rude about this, was removed from his job in the first week of the war.

The fact was that the Germans were strong, only by comparison with British weakness. Mr Churchill at any rate was not responsible for the latter, and his funny figures were perhaps only a misguided attempt to spur rearmament. At a pinch, by risking everything, and sacrificing bomb load for fuel, the Germans could have put in an unescorted attack by some 400 bombers. But against this, there were at Scapa eight heavy AA guns, no short-range AA guns, and no high-performance fighters. There was a Naval Air Station at Hatston, outside Kirkwall, but the fighters there were naval machines and, like all naval aircraft, inevitably had a performance much inferior to that of equivalent RAF types; they could not keep up with the fast 'evader' bombers of the *Luftwaffe*, let alone catch them. The only part of the Scapa defences which had not been removed, weakened or neglected in the peaceful years were the tides, which, fortunately, were beyond Government control. The tremendous surge and scour of the unhampered Atlantic – for nothing but 3,000 miles of water by to the westward – made mining an almost impossible proposition.

To attempt to allocate detailed responsibility for this state of affairs, without having access to all the documents, would be presumptuous. The question is dealt with, to a certain extent, by Captain Roskill in '*The War at Sea.*' He exonerates the officers on the spot, who had reported the deficiencies; passes the responsibility to the Admiralty, who had expressed themselves satisfied and at the same time had delayed making up their minds whether or not to use Scapa as the main fleet base; and finally passes it on again to Mr Chamberlain, for dealing a little too timidly with Hitler. There is no reason why it should stop there; responsibility could be taken as far back as Mr Baldwin and spread to include the entire British electorate of the 1930s, less that small portion of it which was actively in favour of rearmament. It could hardly be said that the labour force was lacking – during that period there were between one and three million unemployed rotting out their lives in despair. The fact is that hardly anyone wanted war with Germany, except one or two limelight-seeking politicians and a handful of fanatics who camouflaged their possibly subconscious desires under hysterical calls for peace and 'collective security.' The consequent political confusion resulted in Britain getting the worst of all possible solutions – a world war, without the means to wage it properly.

There were, of course, similar stresses and strains inside Germany; with the difference that the man in charge was an excitable, hypnotic Bavarian peasant, a master of mass publicity but quite lacking in all the qualities needed to walk the dangerous tightrope he had chosen to negotiate.

On the day he finally fell off it, the officers of the *Royal Oak* were assembled on the quarterdeck to drink a toast, 'Damnation to the enemy.' Shortly afterwards Winston Churchill, who had now got back into the public eye as First Lord of the Admiralty, came on board and made a speech. Until then, there had been a certain air of unreality about the war. One of his listeners, Stanley Saltmarsh, said afterward, 'To me, as a young Marine, it was frightening; but I felt if I stuck to my training, I'd get through. Probably for the first time, I thought of God and religion.'

The *Royal Oak* now had an Admiral and his staff aboard, and her crew was being brought up to full wartime complement. Rear-Admiral H E C Blagrove had recently been appointed Admiral Superintendent of Chatham Dockyard, but the outbreak of war meant for him a welcome opportunity to command a Battle Squadron.

Among his staff, who also joined at this time, were Flag-Lieutenant G

Affleck-Graves and 'Bertie' Pyne, who was his Chief Writer. Most of the Marines were very young, with not more than eighteen months service, so some thirty three-badge men were drafted to the ship, among them McLaverty, whose service went back to beyond the first world war. At the other end at the age-scale, Cadet P H Owen found his course of cadets recalled from leave and some of them sent to Scapa; after a few days in the *Iron Duke*, he joined the *Royal Oak*. Paymaster Commander J R Cundall joined in September – on his birthday.

As the last shots of the Polish campaign died away, Hitler turned his attention to the main enemy – the British fleet. He could not match it at sea in a direct action because his main interest, which lay in an eventual drive by great armies to the eastward, had prevented him from building anything like adequate numbers of ships. He was weak even in submarines. But, as the former High Seas Fleet had been scuttled – in Scapa Flow – what he did have were mostly new, whereas what the Royal Navy had were mostly old. Additionally, a German warship built for limited-length operations in the North Sea and Atlantic would always have a certain 'edge' over a British warship, designed to serve for years at a time in all climates, in which crew comfort was necessarily a larger consideration. A carefully integrated campaign in which surface warships, submarines, mines and aircraft all played a part, might be able to knock out within a few months a useful proportion of the British Home Fleet. By then, he hoped to use his armies to take for him forward bases in Holland, Belgium and Northern France, from which a war of attrition on British sea communications could be waged at short range, resulting if all went well in a peace by negotiation with Britain and France. He would then be free to achieve his lifelong dream in the East.

He did not then anticipate that his limited objectives campaign in the West would be delayed until the following year and that, when it finally took place, it would result in the total overthrow of all Allied forces on the continent.

On 6th September the first reconnaissance flight over Scapa was made, by a weather aircraft of Air Fleet II; and on the 7th the Admiralty warned Admiral Forbes, then with the Home Fleet at Scapa, that an attack by 800 bombers was possible. The photograph taken on the 6th, which showed both the main fleet anchorage and the destroyer anchorage, with the ships in them, reached the desk of Commodore Dönitz, commanding the U-boat arm, on 11th September. Dönitz wanted more information, and on the 13th sent out U-14 to patrol the Orkneys and report on the floating defences, the coast defences and the currents. When it got back, on the 29th, its captain said that he thought that a U-boat could penetrate Hoxa Sound when the 'gate' was open. More reconnaissance aircraft flew over Scapa, so high that the sound of their engines could not be heard, out of range of the AA guns and beyond the reach of the naval fighters.

During the month, Lieutenant B Keen, RM, was ordered to take about twenty-five Marines from the *Royal Oak* over to Kirkwall as a guard for some German prisoners. The prisoners turned out to be the entire crew of U-39, which, on 14th September, had put in an ineffective attack against the aircraft carrier *Ark Royal*, then at sea with part of the Home Fleet. After being counter-attacked, the U-boat had blown her tanks and come to the surface, to the disgust of some of her crew. The U-boat captain expected to be allowed to go shopping in Kirkwall. After two days, Lieutenant Keen and his Marines took the prisoners on board the fleet minesweeper *Hebe* and, during the passage from Scapa to Scrabster, some of the Germans showed great familiarity with the Pentland Firth, pointing out various landmarks quite correctly. Obviously, Scapa was being kept under close observation from both sea and air. The prisoners were eventually handed over to the Army at Inverness.

By that time, the Germans had more than evened the score. U-29 sank the aircraft carrier *Courageous* west of Ireland on 17th September. However, it was not very long before the Home Fleet again provided Lieutenant Keen with some more work to do. Once again the bait had been the *Ark Royal* which, with two battleships, was escorting home from enemy waters a damaged British submarine. This gave the Germans the opportunity they wanted, to try out their air force at close range on heavy units of the Home Fleet. At eleven o'clock on the morning of 26th September, naval reconnaissance aircraft saw that the force was being followed – three Dornier 18 flying boats were shadowing it from a distance. The *Ark Royal* turned into wind and flew off nine Skuas, which were slower than the flying boats they were to attack. However, they put one down into the sea and the destroyer *Somali* picked up the crew. Very shortly after that, a single German aircraft dived out of the clouds onto the *Ark Royal* and planted a 2,000-lb bomb thirty yards from the bow, which caused a cascade of water to fall on the flight deck. The pilot did not in fact claim to have sunk her, but the Propaganda Ministry did; they subsequently issued a booklet, supposed to have been written by the pilot, entitled 'How I Sank the *Ark*

Royal.' Their next in that line was to be a book, attributed to a U-boat commander, entitled 'I Sank the *Royal Oak.*' In both cases, the date was right.

This time, Lieutenant Keen, who spoke no German, found that one of the Germans from the flying boat spoke excellent English; he had been educated in England and possessed English connections. During the two or three days they had to wait at Kirkwall, this German invited Keen, quite seriously, to spend a ski holiday with him later that year. He judged that the French had no taste for the war and would soon pack it in; and a compromise peace would probably follow. The captain of U-39, it will be recalled, had also regarded the war as a non-serious matter, certainly not serious enough to prevent him from being allowed to go shopping in Kirkwall. McLaverty came out of it best of all, for one of the Germans, whose name he thought might be spelt Hinkenbein, gave him his Mae West. It was even more beautiful than the original, and self-inflating, with an oxygen bottle one side and a whisky flask the other.

The object of the stay at Kirkwall was to await the arrival of still more prisoners, this time from the blockade-runner *Minden*, which had failed to break through the Northern Patrol. Her crew, curiously enough, consisted of about thirty Germans and some three dozen Chinese. On delivering this lot to the *Hebe*, at about two in the morning, Keen found her First Lieutenant with his wits sufficiently about him to reply, 'Sorry, no can do; not enough rice.'

At about the same time, two pocket battleships had broken out into the Atlantic; to draw off pursuit, the Germans decided to create a diversion in the North Sea. They sent out the battle-cruiser *Gneisnau* and the cruiser *Köln*, with nine destroyers. Anything small they could smash, anything heavy they could run away from; and when they ran away, it was to be towards the Skagerrak, where a U-boat and *Luftwaffe* reception would be laid on. On 8th October the force was sighted off Lister Light, on the Norwegian coast, by an aircraft of Coastal Command. The Home Fleet sailed from Scapa, split into groups to cover the various courses which the German force might steer. The battle-cruisers *Hood* and *Repulse*, old but fairly fast, formed the bulk of one group; the battleships *Nelson* and *Rodney*, with the aircraft carrier *Furious*, formed the core of another. The *Royal Oak* was much too slow to keep up with either of these forces and was sent to patrol the Fair Isle Channel with an escort of two destroyers. The weather was extremely bad. The gale howled in from the Atlantic and the *Royal Oak* went wallowing through it, looking like an outsize submarine with only the conning-tower showing. Closed up at Number 2 gun of the starboard six-inch battery was Stanley Saltmarsh, who had been in the Marines four years and had never been seasick. He was now. The only thing he could keep down were apples. There was a terrible mess in the battery, the gundeck was afloat most of the time, several of the guns were damaged and jammed in traverse. Carley rafts were torn away or wrecked; and the two escorting destroyers vanished in the murk, losing contact completely. When the battleship turned at the end of her patrol line and came back again, the raging seas put the port battery completely out of action, emphasising the tight-lipped comment in *Jane's* on this class, 'They are fine ships, but suffer rather from reduced freeboard.'

For the men, it was misery, particularly as they had only a hazy idea of what it was all in aid of; but the feelings of the senior officers can barely be imagined. In good weather the poor old battleship cruised at twelve knots; when pushed, and rattling in every plate, she could just make eighteen knots. And she was now alone, without any escort whatever. A fine crew, almost all of them professionals, with many irreplaceable long-service men among them, were virtually wasting their time in a wacked-out old battlewagon which should have been replaced by a modern ship years before.

On 10th October, Admiral Forces – who had yet to sight the German ships – was told that they were returning to harbour. It was hardly surprising, in the circumstances, that Coastal Command had lost contact with them for some time and that the Home Fleet had been searching blind; the acid quality of the naval historian's comments on the RAF seem hardly justified. On that day the operation was abandoned and most of the Home Fleet set course for Scapa.

They had barely arrived when a German reconnaissance aircraft flew over. The crew of the *Royal Oak* were so worn out with lost sleep and the struggle in the gale that they hardly noticed it, or at what time it appeared, but only that the battle-cruiser *Repulse* was then anchored a short distance away from them, in the direction of Kirkwall. From German records it appears that this was the aircraft flown by Lieutenant Newe which took a number of excellent pictures at three p.m. on Thursday, 12th October. Imprinted on one negative must have been the outlines of the *Royal Oak* and the *Repulse*, anchored close together in the north-east corner of the Flow; and that picture was indelibly fixed on German minds thereafter.

But, after dark, the Home Fleet left the known insecurity of Scapa for its temporary bases in Scotland; with it, went the *Repulse*. The only major operational unit left behind was the *Royal Oak* – too slow to keep up, but still useful as a floating anti-aircraft battery. The ship carried eight four-inch AA guns, as well as an array of short-range weapons; the guns' crews, under Lieutenant-Commander Roper and Petty Officer Stannard, had been well-trained in the last six months and would give a good account of themselves if the heavy air attack, which the Admiralty believed was being planned, should actually take place.

CHAPTER THREE

'Unlucky for Some'

On Friday the 13th of October, most of the officers and men of the *Royal Oak* were looking forward to a full night in – off watch, and in harbour; some hoped to get a few hours ashore. But a hard day lay ahead for most of them, repairing damage and storing ship.

That morning Lieutenant Keen went over to the *Iron Duke* for mail in the fishing drifter *Daisy II*. It was a trip he always enjoyed. The 'Iron Duck' lay off Lyness, ten miles away, and there was plenty of time for a really heavy breakfast. The six-man crew of the drifter, all civilians, usually had four eggs, with lashings of bacon – eggs were always plentiful in Orkney throughout the war. The Master of the *Daisy* was Skipper John G Gatt; a tall, burly man from Aberdeenshire, he was part-owner of the vessel, which was a big modern steam drifter of steel construction. She had been taken over by the Admiralty just after the outbreak of war and on 17th September had been detailed to attend on the *Royal Oak* whenever she was in Scapa. She acted as a son of waterborne bus-cum-lorry, equally capable of taking liberty men ashore or bringing stores alongside. But, this morning, the job was mail.

The drifter passed the main fleet anchorage, some miles south of where the *Royal Oak* was lying, and ran in between the islands of Fara and Flotta, the bare, purple and brown hills of Hoy ahead. This part of Hoy, inside the

Flow, was low-lying and actually boasted a coastal road, but the interior was mountainous and trackless, some of the hills rising to over 1,500 feet. Some of them had curiously descriptive names, such as Whitefowl Hill and the Red Hill of Sneuk. Almost ahead lay Lyness, an untidy straggle of huts and oil tanks, topped by the cool white cross of the naval cemetery. Many of the dead from Jutland lay buried there, as well as Germans from the surrendered High Seas Fleet.

To starboard was a long stretch of water which served as the destroyer anchorage; a number of coasters, acting as fleet auxiliaries, were anchored there, as well as two destroyers. A little further north, opposite the island of Rysa, lay the battle-cruiser *Derfflinger*, bottom up, the last of the German ships to be raised by Cox & Danks. To port was Switha Sound, with a boom draggled in the water between Flotta and Hoy; that particular part of Hoy was where the Norsemen first settled. In the Sagas, it is called Vagaland. There was here a great bay, like a fiord, which ran for five miles into the interior of Hoy. Its name was Longhope. Clustered around its mouth were two sizable ships, the ex-Lamport & Holt liner *Voltaire*, acting as a depot ship, and the hospital ship *Saint Abba*.

Anchored inside Longhope, close to the northern shore, was the *Iron Duke*, partly demilitarised, with two of her turrets removed. The place of the after tunet was taken by a hut – which was the post office. She acted as a headquarters ship and, less romantically, detention centre. All these ships were necessary, because there were hardly any houses, there was nothing one could even call a village. In summer, there were more seals than humans sunbathing on the beaches.

But even in July, anyone who dived straight in, without first getting used to the water, would come up with a scream, numbed with the shock. The Arctic Circle was not so very far away.

After her visit to the *Iron Duke*, the *Daisy* spent the rest of the morning helping to store the *Royal Oak*. As well as naval stores from Lyness, there was fresh food from Kirkwall and frozen food from a store ship. All this had been prepared in advance, ready for her return from sea. Sergeant G H Booth, who was in charge of the party of Marines helping to get the stores aboard, had received in that morning's post a cigarette lighter – a gift from his wife, Evelyn. Supply Petty Officer N J Finley, who was superintending the work, had less reason to be pleased – some of the rum was leaking. Leading Store Assistant W G T Batterbury, who was the junior rating of the big Central Stores amidships on the starboard side, had a hard day, as did his equal in rank, Frank Sims, whose job it was to check the cartons of eggs, butter, meat and so on, which were coming out of the supply ship. The *Royal Oak*, of course, had her own refrigerating plant; about the size of a small drawing room, it was forward, deep down in the ship. Close by, also in the bow, was the inflammable store. When work ended quite a number of the cases were left in the flat outside the stores, so that men going to the forward 'heads' had to walk round them. The same was true of the flat near the after stores, in the vicinity of 'X' turret.

Chief Engine room Artificer C J Wilson who, by virtue of his job, got around the ship quite a lot, noted that stores were being loaded at three points – through the hatch in the forepeak by the torpedo flat (the battleship carried four twenty-one inch torpedo tubes in the bow), by a gangway amidships to the Central Stores, and by another hatch aft of the engine room, by the Marines messdeck and the magazines. What he didn't like was that many of the men coming aboard with stores were civilians; in many cases there was no one even to show them the way, which perhaps was why they simply left some of the stores in the flats. They were all pretty well bound to be Admiralty employees, like the crew of the *Daisy*, but then again, the IRA had recently been in the news for putting bombs in pillar boxes; it was silly to give anyone half a chance. Perhaps it was this or, more likely, some subconscious unease, but Wilson was suddenly seized by a burning desire to get a torch; he determined to buy one in Kirkwall when he went ashore later in the day.

Friday the 13th was also pay day – and unusually large sums passed across the pay table because, in addition to a fortnight's pay, the men's half-yearly settlement was due. They felt rich; and some of them, by 'lights out,' expected to be a good deal richer. But most men wanted to go ashore and there were the usual grumbles because the number free to go was small. Chief Ordnance Artificer E G Dommett, for instance, with the rest of the ordnance staff, was hard at work in the port battery, housing six of the six-inch guns of the secondary armament, which had been damaged in the storm.

After pay parade, which was later than usual, the *Daisy* took the liberty party ashore. It was a fine day, with a light to moderate wind from the N.E.. a great contrast to the gales of the previous days, and there was a particularly lovely sunset, even for Scapa. Among the lucky ones was Stanley Rowlands who had, without his being aware of it, just been promoted Corporal; but he did not discover this until he reported at Eastney after survivor's leave. He went ashore with his chum, Jimmy

James, who was keen to have a studio portrait taken; the picture was sent on in due course, but Jimmy was not there to see it. Stoker H P Cleverley could have gone, but swapped watches with Stoker Johnson, because Johnson was an Orcadian; consequently it was Johnson, not Cleverley, who was down below in the engine room from midnight onwards.

Wilson, when he got ashore, set out at once in search of a torch. He had longer at his disposal than the ratings, who would be taken back in the *Daisy* at eight p.m. But, because of the blackout, torches were in short supply; also it was late for a shopping expedition. In the end, he got hold of a damaged torch, which he bought for a nominal sum; then, in great good humour, he put through a telephone call to his wife. She sounded worried. There had been news of air raids on ships in the North Sea. 'Where are you, dear?' she asked.

'Can't tell you,' joked Wilson, 'but we're as safe as houses!'

Earlier in the afternoon some of the senior officers landed on the shore opposite where the *Royal Oak* was anchored and went for a walk along the cliffs in the direction of the village of St Mary's and the channel where the blockships were lying. Captain Benn and Paymaster Commander Cundall did not get very far, but Cundall thought that the blockships must have moved, the gap was so large. Engineer Commander J W Renshaw and Surgeon Commander G L Ritchie, MC, went further, and began to remark on the wide gap between the nearest blockship and the shore. It seemed to Renshaw that there was ample room for a ship of destroyer size to get through. However, they thought nothing more of it, assuming that the gap was watched, either from the shore or by a patrolling drifter.

When Wilson came back in the *Daisy* at nine p.m., he went below to help the watch on duty in the engine room. They were getting up steam, because the ship was due to move at seven a.m. next day. The decision had been taken at a staff conference held a few hours previously. Intelligence had indicated that an air attack on Scapa Flow was impending and some of the Lieutenant-Commanders had pointed out that the ship's present berth was too vulnerable; they urged that the *Royal Oak* should either go to sea or move to the main fleet anchorage, where a few anti-torpedo nets were already in position. Other officers opposed this and Admiral Blagrove, who was still new to the ship, had finally decided to move on the following day.

Rumours of the impending air attack somehow got round and Leading Seaman H J Instance, who was earning an extra 8d. a day as an Assistant Schoolmaster, found that some of the 120 Boys (aged 14-17) carried by the

Royal Oak were taking this very seriously, coupling with it the ill-omen of the date. He tried to allay their fears. However, those who had heard the nine o'clock news were in great good humour. The BBC were reporting Friday the 13th as unlucky for the Germans – two U-boats had been sunk. [1]

The first watch had gone on duty an hour before – at eight p.m. As the ship was in harbour, liable only to air attack, the AA guns' crews were closed up. Lieutenant C E L Sclater, as HA Control Officer, was on the bridge. Cadet Owen was at his air defence position – halfway up the tripod. There were a dozen men aloft with binoculars as air lookouts. The AA Pool, which consisted of the spare hands of the watch who, in emergency, would form ammunition supply panics, were sleeping in the port battery; their duty Petty Officer was J R Kerr. As he was also the Divisional Petty Officer, he spent most of the evening in the office, making out lists of names for various working parties which would go ashore the following day. There were also a number of men watching over machinery in various parts of the ship – Leading Stoker T N Jones, for instance, was in the dynamo room, below the waterline near the after magazines. In all, some 200 men out of about 1,200 were on watch, which meant that most of the crew would be able to get a good night's sleep.

After continual watch-keeping at sea – four hours on, four hours off – plus the gale, and then a heavy day repairing damage and storing ship, many of them were, like Sick Berth Attendant R G Bendell, 'pretty near Bakers.' Bendell should have remained dressed, but he took a chance and turned in soon after nine p.m.

The date had definitely proved unlucky for two members of the crew. The *Royal Oak* was a gambling ship, boasting a Fraz school, a Shoot school, and a Pontoon school, as well as a Crown and Anchor school. Play normally took place in the Gaming Space, commonly known as 'Monte Carlo,' actually the canteen. A rare break-down of security in the all-important Lookout system had occurred, and the 2 i/c of the Fraz school had been caught by a member of the ship's police. Together with a Marine, he was now in cells forward, with an armed Marine sentry outside the locked door. The Navy, in common with the other Services, takes a poor view of gambling, observing justly that men who have so little money cannot afford to hazard it on games of chance.

[1] This report was followed at ten o'clock by another claim: 'With reference to the previous communiqué the Admiralty state that information had just been received of destruction of a third U-boat today, Friday, October 13. In this case also the hunting craft were able to rescue a few survivors.' Churchill, in his memoirs, states that these reports were 'not confirmed by the post-war analysis'; that they came in while he was dining, for the first time, with the Prime Minister; and that Mrs Chamberlain most charmingly suggested that he had arranged all this for their especial benefit.

It was ten p.m. before Skipper Gatt and his crew, who had brought back the last liberty party, could turn in. They secured the *Daisy* by bow and stern lines to the port side of the battleship, forward of the accommodation ladder leading to the quarterdeck and aft of the last gun in the battery. When it returned from the *Iron Duke*, the steam picket boat would tie up to the boom ahead of them; secured already to the boom on the other side of the ship was the big motor launch. All other boats were inboard, including the Captain's gig, which was aft on the quarterdeck, ready to be painted next day.

Supply Petty Officer Finley was playing *Monopoly* in the small mess set aside for Supply and Cook Petty Officers. At ten-thirty the last record was played over the ship's broadcasting system. As usual, it was 'Goodnight, My Love.' Finley finished his game and went up to the Supply Office, where he slept, fortunately for him. No one came alive out of that mess. The only other survivor of the group was Petty Officer Cook G Calder, who was on watch.

Sergeant Booth was going round the ship, seeing to it that all deadlights were secured and all seadoors closed; he turned in at about eleven p.m., partly dressed, because he was Second Duty. Leading Seaman T W Blundell had just been promoted to Acting Petty Officer; the other cox and crew were out tonight in the picket boat, collecting mail from the *Iron Duke*, so he was making the most of his new mess, to get in a quiet game of Pontoon. Petty Officer Kerr, having completed the rosters for the next day, left the Divisional office and followed his usual routine of dropping in at the Police office for a chat with RPO Williams and Acting/RPO Bealing. By that time, the mail had arrived, so he took it to the mess, where he found only PO Scarff and PO Oxley. That was the last he saw of the mess and PO Oxley. At about eleven-fifteen p.m. he returned to the office and turned in. The 'Guest Night' which had been going on in the Gunroom broke up at about that time, because the junior officers would have to be up early next morning, in view of the fact that the ship would be shifting to another berth at seven a.m.

In the officers' quarters aft Lieutenant Michael Benton, RM, had turned in early, but a small group were still in the Wardroom, playing Double Cameroon, a game in which ten dice are used. In one straight throw. Lieutenant Keen got nine Jacks and a Queen. 'Now who's Friday the 13th unlucky for!'

He took out a cigarette and lit it. Immediately, two other officers asked him for a light, because they were short of matches and the bar was now shut. Keen gave a light to a Schoolmaster and then to Surgeon-Lieutenant Dickie, asking him if he minded being third. He didn't. An hour or so later he was dead.

At midnight the watches changed over. Cadet Owen came down from his air defence position halfway up the tripod and turned into his hammock in the Officers' Cabin flat, just aft of the Marines' messdeck. Lieutenant Sclater went to his cabin, which was right aft, under the Admiral's quarters. Leading Signalman W J Fossey came onto the bridge, relieving an Isle of Wight man, Leading Signalman Bun. It was a dark night, he noticed; he could just make out the cliffs some six cables away on the starboard side as a faintly darker mass than the sky; but, apart from that, there was nothing at all visible.

Stoker H P Jones, who had been in the dynamo room, was relieved by Leading Stoker Watson; Jones went to the officer of the watch for permission to open the armoured water-tight door leading to the bathroom. After all the stokers who had just come off watch had had a bath, he closed the water-tight door, and reported it closed to the officer of the watch. By this time it was getting on for one a.m., Saturday, the 14th. He got into his hammock, picked up two pages of an old daily newspaper which was lying around, and began idly to read through them.

The little party of officers in the Wardroom had finished their game about fifteen minutes before. Lieutenant Keen collected the three letters which had just arrived for him and, after he had got into bed, settled down in peace to read them.

CHAPTER FOUR

'DON'T WORRY – IT'S SATURDAY THE 14TH!'

A one o'clock on the morning of Saturday, 14th October, Leading Signalman Fossey had been on duty on the Bag-deck for an hour. He began to shift the 'challenges,' the code letters used for challenging other ships. First he altered those on the starboard side, then those on the port side. When he had finished, he looked at the clock. It showed 1.04 a.m.

Precisely at that moment there was an explosion forward. The flag-deck was part of the bridge, with a good view forward over 'B' and 'A' turrets to the bow, but Fossey saw no cascade of water up the side, which one would expect from a torpedo hit, especially in shallow water. He at once assumed that an aircraft had glided down over them, engines shut off, and that the explosion was from a bomb. On the heels of the explosion came a thunderous, rumbling roar, painful to the ears; the anchor cables were running out, out of control. That seemed to confirm the bomb impression; the cables were led inboard to a point on the forecastle well back from the bow and on the centre line of the deck. He reached for a signal pad and wrote down the time of the occurrence.

Most of those who were sleeping forward of the bridge were woken up. Chief E R A Wilson, whose hammock was well forward, under the torpedo flat, heard an 'almighty bang' which seemed to come from right underneath, followed by the roar of the cables running out overhead. He got up at once, took off his pyjamas, put on his underwear, added the pyjamas as an afterthought, then a pair of overalls, shoes and cap. Rough-and-ready dressed, he came out into the torpedo flat, clutching his torch.

Able Seaman A J Farley, who had been sleeping in 'A' space, on the lowest deck down under 'A' turret, opened his eyes, rubbed them, and thought he was dreaming. A steel shelf near his hammock had been snapped in two. He pulled on his trousers and climbed to the deck above, where some ratings told him they thought it was an air raid. But no alarm rattles had been sounded, so he climbed up another deck yet and stood outside the Sick Bay. The deckhead of the forecastle was gaping apart at the top and there were fumes about which had a very sickly smell. But all the lights were on. He thought the indications pointed to an internal explosion in the Inflammable Store.

Chief Stoker A Lawrence was not merely woken up by the explosion, he was pitched out of his hammock by it. He sat on the deck for a moment, dazed and still sleepy, then was away up the ladder to the deck above, just under and slightly forward of 'A' turret. He could hear a man screaming, somewhere forward of that, and saw that there was water escaping – a fine spray was being blown about, as if from a burst pipe. Then it dawned on him that the *Royal Oak* was in harbour. The explanation perhaps was some explosion in the Paint Store or a CO_2 bottle in the refrigeration plant. That was where the screaming seemed to be coming from, and he made his way towards it.

Leading Seaman Instance slept in a mess about ten feet forward of the Boys' messdeck. The explosion woke most of them. Instance himself jumped straight out of bed, ran aft to the bulkhead and looked at the clock – it showed 1.04. He came back, calling out, 'Don't worry – it's Saturday the 14th!' Then, as leading hand of the mess, he told them all to get out of their hammocks and get dressed, ready for action stations. The general impression was that they had been hit by a bomb from a high-flying aeroplane.

The explosion was felt more violently aft than it was forward; 'the stern kicked about as though in a heavy seaway.' Quite a number of officers flung on a coat over pyjamas and dashed up on deck. Cadet Owen, rather bewildered, went to his air defence station under the armoured deck; found it empty, and came back again. Lieutenant Benton, who had taken sandwiches with him to his cabin, in order to get early to bed, was still sleepy. He lay there drowsily, his mind going back to the German reconnaissance plane which had flown over them. 'By Jove, that's a lucky one,' he thought. But there was no drone of aero engines, only a number of orders broadcast on the ship's loudspeaker and a jangle of keys as someone ran forward.

Skipper Gatt, in the *Daisy*, was also woken by the explosion. He jumped out of his bunk and went on deck immediately, to find the officer of the watch, a Marine, asking him what had happened. Gatt hazarded that it might have been one of the fifteen-inch guns firing; the officer said he thought it might have been something in the drifter. When Gatt denied it, a midshipman was sent forward to find out.

When Gatt was talking to the officer, he noticed something floating between the drifter and the *Royal Oak*; it was coming from the bow with the set of the tide. The officer of the watch gave an order for an Aldis lamp to be turned on it, so a midshipman went forward to the flag-deck and told Fossey to illuminate it. Fossey, believing that there were aircraft about, was reluctant. He replied, shortly, that he had a wife and child.

Captain Benn and Commander Nichols came on deck almost simultaneously, together with other senior officers. Someone asked if anyone had heard an aeroplane. Someone else noticed that the explosion had blown down a light-excluding ventilator from the Wardroom and that light was showing. There was a shout for a man to replace it. Commander Nichols began to issue a stream of orders: for the *Daisy* to raise steam, for the picket boat to raise steam, for the launch to be called away. As Skipper Gatt's men tumbled out of their bunks to obey, the ship's broadcasting system began to call: 'Away launch's crew'; 'Magazine Panics take magazine temperatures.'

The latter order sent Lieutenant Moore below, under the armoured deck, together with the special temperature party, the gunners' mates of the turrets, and the gunners' yeomen. The order was a precaution against a magazine explosion, but it sent them all to their deaths.

Captain Benn went forward with a fairly large team, to investigate. It included the second Supply Officer, Lieutenant-Commander McLean, who was responsible for the store rooms; Lieutenant-Commander Roper, the Gunnery Officer; and the Chief Shipwright. Commander Nichols was delayed for a few minutes on the quarter-deck, giving essential orders and talking to Admiral Blagrove, who wanted to know what had happened. The officer of the watch, returning from forward, reported that the slip of the starboard cable had parted; the cable had run out to a 'clench.' Then

Commander Nichols went forward. Other senior officers were making their way forward independently.

Lieutenant-Commander Gregory, the Navigator, came on to the flag-deck, where Fossey and the midshipman had now been joined by the searchlight crews. He was a sharp little man, who missed nothing in his own department and little outside; when he told Fossey to switch on a twenty-inch searchlight, Fossey obeyed. Played on the water on the port side, it showed up what looked to Fossey to be the sort of straw in which whisky bottles are wrapped. Looking down on it from the quarterdeck, Lieutenant Keen noticed something white floating among it – a seagull, or possibly a sailor's cap. Skipper Gatt, much lower down, saw now that it was a mass of straw and pieces of wood. Then the searchlight was switched off.

A number of officers went forward from their quarters through the Marines' messdeck, where Stanley Saltmarsh and his friend Barry Hawes had both got up. Others, like Stanley Rowlands and William Owens, never got up at all; they simply lay awake in their hammocks. As the officers went through, one of them called out, 'Sar'nt-Major, see everybody gets turned back in their hammocks.' Saltmarsh obediently got back and tucked himself up under the blankets; so did Hawes.

In the Marine Sergeants' Mess, one deck lower, the explosion had been felt more violently. G E T Parham, a gunnery instructor, found the ship shaking so much that his head hit the deckhead. He got up and tried to wake the other men, but was told, even by his pal. Bob Bottomley, to shut up and go back to bed. 'I don't believe in getting caught with my pants down,' said Parham, 'so I dressed and went on deck.' It was cold there, and there was no sign of anything wrong, so he came down again and lit a cigarette, waiting.

Sergeant Booth's awakening was equally violent – he found himself suddenly on the deck, and got up angrily, thinking that someone had been skylarking. But no one had. Being Second Duty, he was already half-dressed, so he went up into the Commander's lobby where a number of seamen were queuing to use the night 'heads.' They were talking about an explosion forward, and Booth thought at once of the two men locked in the cells. He tried to get there by going through the Seamen's mess-deck, but there was so much smoke that it was impossible. Because there were so few hatches to the upper deck, he had to retrace his steps before finding a ladder. He went up that, then walked right forward to the foremost hatch in the bows. Below decks there was so much smoke, and such a pungent smell to it, that Booth thought at first that a torpedo warhead had exploded. There was no one in the cell flat – both prisoners had gone, and the sentry, too. Thick, yellow smoke was coming up between the deckplates. The torpedo warheads were down there, and also the refrigerating machinery with its explosive CO_2 bottles; he made his way aft, rapidly, through the Seamen's messdeck from which the smoke was now clearing.

Sergeant McLaverty had turned in about thirty minutes before the explosion. As the duty watch came running forward, McLaverty put his head over the side of his hammock and said, 'What's up?'

'Flood in the cable locker flat.'

That meant trouble right forward in the ship, where the cells were, so McLaverty jumped out and went to find the Marine officer of the watch, Acting/Lieutenant J T E Vincent, who had been in the ship only about a week. 'Look here, sir,' said McLaverty, ' if there's a flood in the cable locker, it may flood the cells as well. Shall I release the prisoners?'

Vincent said that he could, so McLaverty hurried forward through the port battery. There he met the Regulating Petty Officer, coming aft with the two prisoners and the Marine sentry. The screaming which Chief Stoker Lawrence had heard was actually one of these men hammering on the door and shouting to be let out. 'You're released from arrest,' said McLaverty. Then he turned to the sentry. 'Take off your belt and bayonet and look after yourself now.' Crime, or at any rate minor Service crime, sometimes pays; one of the prisoners normally slept in the boat hoist flat with Marine Sandford and a number of others who were killed. But the bad boy survived.

McLaverty hurried back to Lieutenant Vincent, reported the release of the prisoners, then went into the Marines' messdeck, which was directly below the after turrets. 'Come on, lads, get dressed – out of your hammocks!'

'What – another flipping air raid!'

There were groans of protest. Then McLaverty picked, as an example, on fifteen-year-old John Priestley, a Boy Bugler. For three generations, his family had had at least one member serving in the Marines. The Boy was still sleeping soundly, so McLaverty stood him on his feet, gave him a slap round the ears to wake him up, and told him to get on deck. He never saw him again.

Amidships, the explosion had not sounded very loud or important and the shaking of the ship, as the cables ran out, was not nearly so pronounced as at the stern. Also, the men were very tired. Petty Officer Kerr thought the noise was 'like a large zinc bath dropping onto the deck of the Wardroom bathroom.' When Petty Officer Puddy told him he had heard that a CO_2 bottle had blown up, Kerr went into the port battery and saw the AA Pool turned out, in case a fire or cable party was needed. Just forward of the battery was a small mess for Supply staff. Leading Supply Assistant F G Sims woke up, but not at all violently, if he had been in a destroyer instead of a battleship he would have assumed that they had been bumped by another ship – that was the sort of metallic sound it was. But the *Royal Oak* shook – and that made him think. She was 29,000 tons.

He simply lay awake, listening, as did the next man to him; the rest seemed to be asleep. Then the group of senior officers passed through, on their way forward, and he sang out to a seaman, 'What's the panic?'

'Think it's an explosion in the inflammable store.'

In the same mess, LSA Batterbury was also awake; when a call came for the duty Supply rating to go forward, that meant him. Taking with him the keys of the stores, he reported to Petty Officer 'Wiggy' Bennett, who was standing by the trunk leading down to the inflammable store; with him were a number of officers.

In the starboard battery the explosion was similarly vague, so vague that some of the Boys sleeping in the first three gun casemates did not recognise it as such. The running out of the cables or the piped orders which followed were what woke most of them. Seventeen-year-old A W Scovell wondered if he ought to get up – he was the Gunnery Officer's messenger. 'If they want you they'll pipe,' said George White, from the next hammock. One or two Boys got out, but when word reached them that the Admiral and Captain were already forward, investigating, they turned in again.

The deck below the starboard battery was divided into two messes – boys under the first three guns, stokers under the three after guns. That was duplicated under the port battery – with communications ratings forward and more stokers aft. A cross passage connected the two stokers' messdecks. In the communications' mess, not a man got up. Leading Telegraphist R S Jones felt only a muffled bang and a slight vibration; one or two men stirred around in their hammocks, that was all.

When Chief E R A Wilson came into the stokers' messdeck, he found a similar reaction there. After getting rough-and-ready dressed he had gone out, clutching his torch, into the torpedo flat, where there was a strong smell of burning rapeseed oil. This was used for the emergency lamps and was kept in the inflammable store, below the waterline. There was no alteration in the trim of the ship so, if she had been holed, it must have been well forward. In the torpedo flat he found Engineer-Commander J W Renshaw with one of his warrant officers. 'What do you think's wrong, Chiefy?' said Renshaw. Before they had time to discuss it, a seaman reported that the refrigerating machinery had blown up. Renshaw knew that was impossible. 'Get the Salvus apparatus,' he said to Wilson, 'then go down and see what's happened.'

The apparatus, a kind of smoke helmet, was kept in the Central Stores amidships. On his way there, and back, he had to pass through the stokers' messdeck. Almost all of them were lolling in their hammocks, with their heads over the side, not taking very much interest. He suggested they get up, but no enthusiasm was shown. Danger or no danger, they would not stir, except on a direct order.

Until then, they were content to 'leave it to Chiefy.'

In the starboard stokers' messdeck. Leading Stoker Jones did get up; having just come off watch, he was more awake than the others, had indeed been awake, reading, at the time of the explosion. He went aft through the bulkhead and climbed up into the starboard battery, where a number of men were coming from forward. 'It's full of smoke forward,' said one man, 'you can't go that way.' Another added that a CO_2 bottle had exploded. Jones queued at the 'heads,' found the queue too long, and turned in again. All the others were back in their hammocks, except for half a dozen stokers hanging about idly, waiting for something to happen.

Even forward of the bridge, there was not much alarm; the explosion had seemed violent only to those sleeping low down in the ship, near the bows. Wilson had been alarmed, and so had Able Seaman Farley. Farley had come up from 'A' Space, and was standing by the Sick Bay, which was between 'A' and 'B' turrets, on the starboard side. Commander Nichols came along, with the Master-at-Arms, and others; Farley heard him say, 'Get the men turned in, it's only a CO_2 bottle gone up.' The Master-at-Arms came up to the little group of men clustered by the Sick Bay. 'Away you go, lads, it's nothing startling, turn in.'

Chief Ordnance Artificer Dommett slept on the starboard side forward, under the cable, but even he awoke 'dreamily,' gradually becoming conscious of people hurrying about and of an 'evil smell.' He got up, promised two or three drowsy people in the mess to tell them what had happened, and went forward, where Commander Nichols and the Chief Shipwright were already on the scene. The urinals were shattered and there was chaos in the 'heads' generally. The Chief Shipwright tested by holding his hand to the mouths of the vent pipes which led to the spaces below in the bow. It was impossible for him to hold his hand there, because of the air pressure coming out. He reported that the ship was holed and taking water. That looked like an internal explosion in the paint shop or a neighbouring compartment, forward of the collision bulkhead and therefore not at all serious in itself. Anyway, the lights were on; there would be no point in waking the ship for this or even of allowing spectators to crowd round. Dommett and the few others there were advised to return to their messes. Chief Stoker Lawrence, who had been woken much more violently than Dommett, had already done so; after visiting the CO_2 and the 'heads' he had decided that it was nothing serious and saw that the officers and damage control staff were taking action. Engineer Commander Renshaw was on the spot, having been called forward by Captain Benn. Renshaw had first inspected the steering compartment, below the officers' cabin flat but had found nothing wrong. Then he had met Admiral Blagrove who had said, 'Come and look at my pantry.' The cup handles were still hanging from the hooks, but the cups themselves were smashed on the deck; clearly, the ship had had a terrific jolt somewhere. On joining Captain Benn in the bows, he judged quickly that the inflammable store was flooding but that only one compartment was affected and that the flooding could therefore be controlled. He suggested to Captain Benn that the compartments next to the inflammable store should be inspected, to see if the bulkheads were holding, and then gave orders for the water-tight doors leading to the capstan flat to be opened up.

Able Seaman Farley was uneasy; he felt there was more to come. He hung about, many decks down, in 'A' space, then made his decision. When he got back to the Sick Bay, he stood by the door, talking to the solitary patient there. Bendell, the SBA on duty, had never heard the explosion at all; he had been woken by a man who wanted a small cut on his leg dressed. 'How did you do that?' asked Bendell. The man explained that he had been blown out of his hammock. Bendell dressed his cut, took a look outside where there was nothing unusual, except for an odd, cloying smell, and then got back into his cot, 'See the MO in the morning,' said Bendell. 'Don't be a bloody fool,' replied the man, 'the ship's sinking.' Bendell thought he was 'wet,' turned over, and went to sleep.

Supply Petty Officer Finley, who slept in the Victualling office, high up behind 'B' turret, had felt the explosion sufficiently to go down to the main deck, where he heard the ' buzz' about the CO_2 bottle. If true, that was his pigeon – the refrigerator held fourteen days' supply of fresh food. But he found only little wisps of blue smoke from the direction of the cable locker flat and had to put up with jokes about the job he would have in the moming, putting the bits of beef together again.

Batterbury now saw a man go down the trunk – rather like a lift shaft – which led from the upper deck, just forward of the anti-flash screens, to the capstan flat and below-waterline compartments. It was in fact a Chief Stoker sent down by Renshaw. Batterbury thought he was a very brave man, and had the impression he had volunteered. According to Batterbury's recollection, it was at this point that he thought he saw a flash or flame coming up the trunk, certain to engulf the man before he could possibly climb up again. Possibly he may have been confusing the sequence, for the Chief Stoker was doomed, and may well have been the first man to die in the *Royal Oak*. Anyway, Batterbury was sufficiently shaken by whatever it was he saw, to run aft to warn his friends. He burst into the Supply mess, shouting to LSA Hyde, 'Come on, Jekyl, get up, there's trouble forward!'

'Jekyl' made no move to get up. He only grunted sleepily, 'If the ship's going down, put me in the rum tub. I'll drown in rum.'

CHAPTER FIVE

'THE BLOODY SHIP'S GOING TO TURN OVER'

(FORWARD)

At least twelve minutes, but not more than thirteen, had elapsed since the explosion. In that time, the senior officers had dressed, gone forward, and decided that, as the breathing pipe from the inflammable store was freely venting air, that particular compartment was flooding. The inflammable store was a place where a small internal explosion was possible and, indeed. Paymaster Lieutenant Commander Q G S Maclean, responsible for the store, afterwards told Lieutenant Keen that he was at that time thinking up answers for his court martial,

No one could know then that the stem and keel of the ship had been blown away in the paint store area – only divers could ascertain that. Even if it had been known, it would not have indicated mortal injury to the *Royal Oak*. The bow, where the hull is narrow and the compartments small, can take a good deal of damage without even affecting the trim of the ship, as it had in this case. On the evidence available, there was no reason for alarm.

Most of the crew were still in their hammocks, a good many of them asleep; among those who had got up there was a general desire to visit the night 'heads.' which were on the port side, below the Wardroom. Nearby was a hatch leading down to the messdeck and workshops. Dommett joined the queue; well ahead of him were Instance, Able Seaman Hancock, and Ordinary Seaman Hearn. Instance had donned trousers and service jersey; had he not done so, he would not have survived the next thirty seconds.

On the opposite side of the ship Paymaster Commander J R Cundall, who had put on trousers, monkey jacket and scarf over his pyjamas, was walking forward through the starboard battery; he was slightly better protected than Instance, because he had put on his cap. Petty Officer Kerr, who had found the queue at the 'heads' too formidable for him, was standing outside the office, talking to Petty Officer Puddy. Finley was nearby, idly wondering if there was anything for him in the Mail office.

Alongside, in the drifter, Skipper Gatt was still on deck, standing with the cook by the hatch forward. The score or so of officers, who had thrown greatcoats over their pyjamas and come on the quarterdeck, was now reduced to about eight. Among this group, by now rather cold, were Flag-Lieutenant Affleck-Graves, Lieutenant Keen, and Midshipman R P Pirie. Lieutenant C E L Sclater had arrived on deck some time after everyone else, but, on being told it was only an explosion in the paint store, had gone below again. Cadet Owen had been advised to turn in again and Lieutenant Benton, still sleepy, had never got out of his bunk at all.

Directly under the quarterdeck, McLaverty and Booth were trying to wake the Marines. There were sleepy protests of, 'Don't be so bloody wet!' and half of them turned over, and tried to get off to sleep again. Booth sang out, 'Stop arguing the point – everyone out of his hammock!'

At that moment, Lieutenant Keen was standing by the accommodation ladder and looking forward and to starboard. He heard a vague thump and saw a great column of white spray go up as high, if not higher than, the spotting top, apparently almost in line with 'B' turret. The ship shuddered violently and Dommett, outside the 'heads,' saw lamp fittings and bulkheads shaking and moving as if made of cardboard and yet still remain in position. Fossey, on the flag-deck, looked at the clock, reached for the signal pad, and wrote – '1.16.'

Batterbury turned round and ran back to the mess, to be with his pals; Bendell was blown or thrown out of his cot in the Sick Bay; Finley shouted, 'That's no CO_2 room – that's a torpedo!' and ran for the nearest ladder, kicking his shoes off as he did so. Lawrence, several decks down, was pitched out of his hammock and, as he lay there dazed, heard water pouring in and the rumbling of gear as it was swept away by the torrent.

The stokers jumped out of their hammocks, and Jones managed to get through the door in the bulkhead aft and halfway up the ladder. Instance, who was now inside the 'heads' and just about to go out, remarked to Hearn, 'We'll be going back to Pompey for a refit, if this goes on.'

About fifteen seconds later – it may even have been as much as forty-five seconds later – Lieutenant Keen, still standing by the accommodation ladder, heard two almost simultaneous thumps, which might have been two explosions almost together or one very large one. This time, there was no spray – merely a thick black cloud of smoke, with clearly defined edges, drifting slowly towards him. He thought it was probably atomised oil fuel from the tanks on the starboard side. On that, he and the other officers turned and 'ran like riggers' to the back end of the quarterdeck, in case there should be any fragments flying about. Midshipman Pirie, in a narrative published shortly afterwards in the magazine of his old school, Ardvreck, wrote, 'This explosion was much more violent than its predecessors, and a great pall of black smoke hung over the ship. There was also a frightful smell of burnt explosive, and the ship started heeling over quickly.'

This explosion appeared to Pirie to be just forward of the mainmast – and did indeed turn the starboard engine room No. 1 Boiler Room and the Central Stores into a chaos of wreckage, opening them to the sea. The Boys' messdeck and both Stokers' messdecks caught fire, killing most of the boys and a great many of the stokers.

The little group of officers, now right aft on the quarter-deck, got up and began to unship the Captain's gig, which was on its chocks there; it was difficult because the ship, with the utmost deliberation, was rolling slowly over to starboard, shaking and shuddering as the water rushed in and altered her trim from moment to moment. While they were doing this, a final explosion occurred, apparently right under the Marines' messdeck. Skipper Gatt saw the blast of it go right to the maintop, and then another cloud of black smoke rolled up and began to drift towards the little group of officers struggling with the gig. The battleship was now heeled over about 15° to starboard. Within a matter of minutes the sixty-odd 'light-excluding ventilators' on that side would be submerged, with water pouring in through them. On that explosion, too, the lights had failed, so that all below decks was in darkness, except for the glow of the fires; the broadcasting system had been put out of action and the senior officers forward were cut off from all possibility of command. The only senior officer anywhere near the quarterdeck was Paymaster-Commander

Cundall, and he was lying, dreadfully burned, in the starboard battery.

The third explosion had not only caused the lights to fail, but had set an after magazine on fire. The burning cordite did not explode, it simply swept through the vents, seeking the open air. On the starboard side, it caught Leading Stoker Jones as he was halfway up the ladder, then hit Cundall as he was struggling to get out, through the blackout curtains, onto the quarterdeck. On the port side, by the 'heads,' Dommett saw an orange pillar of glittering flame soar up the hatch. He cried, 'Scramble – cordite!' and ran for the quarterdeck. Instance, just coming out of the 'heads,' ducked back inside, but the flame followed him in and swept round and round inside, while he crouched in agony, trying to shield his face and neck. In the Marines' messdeck. Sergeant Booth saw the flame coming at him – 'It was like looking into the muzzle of a blow lamp, the flame was bright orange outside and an intense blue inside.'

The flame roared about inside the ship aft, between the 'heads' and the Marines' messdeck; part of it escaped to the open air through the blackout curtains leading from the port battery onto the quarterdeck, and vanished. Lieutenant Benton, who had leapt out of his bunk, saw, through a partly opened water-tight door leading to the Marines' messdeck, the flame coming at him; but the door was somehow slammed in his face at the last moment. Leading Stoker Jones was knocked off the ladder leading to the lobbies near the quarterdeck by the first sweep of the flame, then was engulfed once more as the flame travelled back.

All this happened, according to many witnesses, within a space of less than a minute; others, including Fossey and Skipper Gatt, who were well clear of the explosions and of the flame, thought there were distinct gaps between explosions, of two minutes or more. The group of officers on the quarterdeck, however, thought the gaps were of about fifteen seconds or so. Inside the ship, men were even more confused, many of them were not even quite sure how many explosions there were. Few, very few, thought they were under attack; the explosions, violent but muffled, were coming from the direction of the store rooms and flats where stores had been put.

Wilson, carrying the Salvus apparatus, had almost reached the torpedo flat when the explosions began. The first lifted the deck underneath him. Blurred, 'as though in a film,' he saw pipes and water beneath his feet. As the last explosion thundered aft. the lights went out, and Wilson felt a great wind which more or less blew him, still on his feet, aft towards the midships galley.

As he went, half blown, half running, it was hard to keep upright. With all dark below, the ship had begun to heel slowly and remorselessly over to starboard. It was hard to find the doors, harder still to open them, because they were no longer vertical. Several times, Wilson found himself across the diagonal of a door before he had reached out to open it. The ship was really turning now, and he knew he had a long way to go. His goal was a ladder by the galley, leading to the upper deck. About forty men were struggling round it; milling, shouting, cursing, unable to see what they were doing.

Wilson was blown at them by the wind, out of the darkness, like a benevolent Buddha, torch in hand. It was the one he had gone to so much trouble to buy. As soon as he flicked it on, the men had no further trouble – 'they went up that ladder like a sea of humanity.' Wilson went up with them; carried up in the rush or blown up by the blast, he seemed not to tread on the ladder at all. Somewhere in this jam was Leading Supply Assistant Sims; when he reached the ladder there was an explosion, and the blast took him right up, as if he were walking on air.

Also in the scrum was Batterbury. The second explosion had sent him running from forward to his chums in the mess, which was near the ladder. He only had a hundred yards to go, but some of the water-tight doors were closed for damage control purposes and others were slamming to with the heel of the ship; it was impossible to go in a straight line.

A door slammed behind him, crushing the head of a man who was trying to get through it. Batterbury saw his eyes and tongue sticking out, then came the sound of the third explosion, and the lights failed. He ran on. The anti-flash curtains in the battery aft were aflame and people were pouring up from the Stokers' messdeck below, 'hollering and howling about men being on fire down there.' This new scrum of men, many of them dazed with horror, scrambled for the ladder. It was, said Batterbury dryly, 'survival of the fittest.' The fear of being trapped inside the heeling ship was overwhelming. Batterbury himself was frantic to get a foot on the ladder.

At the very top of the ladder stood an old man, a Yeoman of Signals or Chief Telegraphist, he thought. Almost certainly, it was Commissioned Telegraphist Hughes-Rowlands, who was generally regarded as being rather ineffective. He was calling out, 'Take it easy... keep steady,' and striking matches to show men the way up. They poured past him into the galley, and made straight for a door leading on to the weather deck. Still the old man stood there, striking his matches, and calling out, 'Keep steady, lads.'

The ship was heeled over to 45° or more now, within a minute or so it must turn completely over and take them with it to the seabed, alive and trapped. Batterbury was still at the bottom of the ladder, shoving and pushing in the scrum. There was the roar of another explosion, the deck-plate simply lifted up, and he went straight up the ladder without touching the rungs at all.

The Chief Stokers' mess, which was on the starboard side under the Sick Bay, was flooded almost at once. Lawrence, blown out of his hammock by the second explosion, could see that the cover of the magazine hatch had been lifted and that water was coming through it. It burst and boiled among the men there and Lawrence, with three others, clung to the ladder to avoid being swept away. As the inrush lost its first momentum. Chief Stoker W R Aplin came floating towards them on a cushion; when he reached the ladder, he calmly stepped off, a lot dryer than they were.

The water trapped at least four men in the cross passage, Lawrence thought, and not all of those with him managed to get up the ladder. Aplin was one; he survived the *Royal Oak*, to lose his life off Norway a few months later.

At the top of the ladder was a flat near the Sick Bay and yet another ladder, which led on to the deck by the forward turrets. Lawrence joined the queue of men beginning to pile up at the bottom of that heeling ladder. The hatch cover above was down, so that those at the top were escaping singly and slowly through the manhole in the centre of it, pushed up by the press from below like corks out of a bottle. None of them thought to stop for a moment and open the main hatch cover, so that a rush of men could get through it; instead, they were running for the side. Even the manhole exit was continually being blocked.

The reason for this was that, just below the hatch cover, was a slab of two-inch armour plate which came out on runners, when a toggle was pulled, just like an extension from a table, to complete the armour protection of the deck. As the heel to starboard increased, so the armour plate began to slide across the opening; to keep it back, someone had to hold down a toggle. That someone, if he stayed too long, was going to lose his life. No one stayed very long; they held down the toggle for a few others to go up, then they left it and joined the queue.

Blundell's hammock was directly under this ladder, but he was one of the last in the queue. He had been dazed by the second explosion, which had caught him as he was reaching for his trousers. 'It was really something. I was in the *Ark Royal* when she was torpedoed in the Mediterranean, but that was nothing in comparison, not the same sort of thing at all. This was as if some giant had got hold of the ship and shook it – a 29,000 ton battleship!'

Bendell, who was at that moment flat on his back on the deck of the Sick Bay, a few yards away, would have agreed. 'It was a hell of a bang – I dreamt about it for ages afterwards.' He simply lay there, for some minutes, stunned.

Able Seaman Farley, who had been at the door of the Sick Bay, was quick off the mark. Already uneasy, even after that minor first explosion, he had marked down an escape route which avoided the ladder. The terrific impact of the second explosion set him off like a runner from the starting pistol. Quickly, he weaved in and out, avoiding dead ends where water-tight doors were shut. A third explosion sent after him a flash, which he saw, and a blast wave, which he felt; it seemed to come from the Boys' messdeck, and put that part of the ship in darkness.

He scrambled up a ladder into the Recreation Space, with not far to go. All mess utensils and gear now began to fall off the tables and roll down the incline of the deck. Down below, he heard a man dashing about in the darkness, bumping into bulkheads, apparently in a blind panic. Farley was afraid, but he was keeping his head; he could not walk to the guardrails at the ship's side, the angle of heel was too steep for that, so he crawled, pulling himself up the deck.

It can have taken him only two or three minutes, but, back at the ladder, men were still struggling and pushing to get up. A hatch in the deck of a warship, exposed to plunging fire, is a weak point, so the number is kept to a minimum. The bulk of her crew – 1,200 men – had only about five minutes in which to funnel themselves through a very small number of openings onto the deck. It simply could not be done. The decision to treat the first explosion as what it appeared to be, however correct it may have seemed at the time, doomed nearly 800 men. They were still in the ship when she rolled over. Some of them never even found the ladders; blundering about in the dark, they lost themselves fatally inside the hull. Others were below the armoured deck and, when the power failed, were unable to open the heavy armoured hatches; completely trapped, they could only wait for the end in darkness. Other men were trapped and pinned, according to survivors and the testimony of divers, by various movable gear inside the ship sliding on to them.

Not less terrifying to the men inside her was the absolute silence. The humming of machinery and fans had ceased; the ship felt dead. And she was going over. 'The steady remorseless rolling over of the ship was a horrible sensation,' said Blundell, 'because you couldn't do a blind thing about it. As we milled round that ladder, with varying degrees of impatience, I remembered the pipe for the magazine parties to go down, and I thought, 'Poor beggars!'

There was a sudden shout of 'Try the ports!'

Most likely. Chief Stoker Lawrence was the man who began it. He had abandoned that ladder the moment the lights went out and made for the Shipwrights' mess, on the port side, opposite the Sick Bay. The scuttles, or port-holes, had 'light-excluding ventilators' in place as a blackout precaution, but they were only plywood. Lawrence worked away at one, to get it free; when an Engineer Officer came to help him, he chased the man away to another port and shouted to a Bos'un or Bos'un's Mate, who came in just then, to pass the word along.

Anyway, at that shout, there was a concerted rush from the ladder, uphill, into the Shipwrights' mess. Blundell, on the tail of the ladder queue, was one of the first here, and with another man he began to undo a ventilator. It was held in place by butterfly nuts. As they worked at it, unscrewing the nuts, the port was coming over above them, and they were leaning backwards.

Bendell was still lying stunned on the inclined deck of the Sick Bay. He came to, still dazed, to see a man with a torch bending over him. It was Sick Berth Petty Officer Henry Main, checking that the Sick Bay was clear of patients and staff. It was, except for Bendell. Main said,

'Get up, she's going,' and, with his torch, led the way to the door.

Neither could walk now, the list was too great. They crawled up the deck, pulling themselves forward with their hands. In the flat outside, the torch was no longer necessary. There was a wall of fire all along the starboard battery and a man shouting that the Boys' messdeck had blown up. Directly below the battery, and above the AA magazine, it was unlikely that anyone could now escape from it.

On the port side they found a ladder leading to a hatch, but the hatch was closed and they could not open it. ' We'll try the POS mess,' said Main, and they crawled on.

They now became separated, probably because Main knew that mess and Bendell did not; instead, he somehow blundered into the pantry next to it. He was now in pitch-darkness, alone, in a strange part of the ship, the only noise being that of men shouting and trampling around, trying to get up ladders or tear open the ventilators.

After the second explosion, which seemed to him like two. Leading Signalman Fossey had logged the time. Then he looked round the flag-deck – it was now empty, except for Signalman Hutchins, his second hand, and the lights were out. He fumbled for the emergency signal lamps, but could not find them; they must have been shaken on to the deck somewhere.

He told Hutchins to go up on the compass bridge to see if he could switch on the masthead lights, then went himself into the signal house and telephoned the signal distributing office. Signalman Hudson answered. Fossey told him to clear the office and tell those in the W/T office nearby that they were to make their way to the upper deck. Then he locked the box with the Confidential Books in it, and placed the key round his neck; shook awake Leading Signalman Harley, who was sleeping in the signal house; and told Hutchins, who had just returned unsuccessfully from the compass bridge, to get into the *Daisy II*.

As Hutchins left, another explosion occurred from aft and Fossey saw two sparks coming out abaft the funnel; he looked at the clock and logged the time – 1.21. Then he heard Commander Nichols calling up from the boat deck, 'Signalman, make a signal for assistance.'

Fossey replied that he could not, as there were no lights working. Then he went back to the signal house, and found Harley still in bed. 'For Christ's sake, turn out, Stripy,' he protested, 'the bloody ship's going to turn over.' With that, the increasing list sent the heavy door of the signal house slamming shut on them – and they were trapped.

When the second explosion occurred and the battleship took on a heavy list. Commander Nichols was aware of what must happen, within minutes, as the sixty or so 'light-excluding' but non-water-tight ventilators on the starboard side were submerged. But the failure of power, shown by the darkness below decks, in effect decapitated the executive officers. General orders could no longer be piped through the broadcast system and the Captain and Commander were reduced to purely local control in whatever part of the ship they happened to be at the time.

What Commander Nichols did was to give orders, as best he could to anyone in the vicinity, to cut free from their lashings all boats and Carley rafts, and anything else that would float. Having left his knife behind, he could not help with that, so went up onto 'B' gundeck where the 'church deals' were stowed; these were long wooden forms used for church parade. As he climbed up, so Lawrence burst open the 'light-exduding ventilator,' to emerge on the ship's side; instead of walking down into the sea, he walked up to 'B' gundeck and recognised Commander Nichols by his voice; all he could see of him was the blurr of a white shin. Together, they grabbed the ends of a 'church deal' and, with a concerted swing, sent it clattering down the side into the water.

Just aft of 'B' turret, two other men were trying to man-handle a Carley raft over the side. One was Leading Seaman E A Boxall, who had escaped from the Boats' Crews mess; the other, thought Boxall, was Lieutenant-Commander Ward, but it was too dark to see properly. The drawback to the Carley raft was its weight and this one, normally needing five or six men, had to be carried up a steeply inclined deck and then manoeuvred over the guardrails. It was an impossible task for just the two of them and, as no one else came to help, the officer said, 'We can't do it on our own – so away you go.' And Boxall went, jumping over the side, with the ship listing at about 45°.

Leading Supply Assistant Batterbury had just been blown up the ladder into the galley, in the superstructure below the gundeck. Here, he started groping around in the dark. 'What are you looking for, chum?' someone asked. 'Me cap,' said Batterbury.

So firm was pre-war naval discipline that the thought uppermost in his mind was that he could not go on deck without a cap. But, bareheaded, he left it and made his way up the heeling deck to the port guardrails. Sitting astride them, fully dressed, with his 'brass hat' on, was a senior officer, he thought Admiral Blagrove, calling out an order to abandon ship to the men working at the Carley rafts and 'church deals.'

Batterbury climbed over the guardrails and walked down the side to the blister, a gigantic swelling from the side of the ship, which was now mostly out of the water. A sailor was sitting down on it, taking his shoes off. Batterhury thought that was sensible, and sat down to do the same. He got one shoe off, then lost his balance and, dressed only in thin vest and pants, went sliding on his back down the seaweed and barnacles towards the water. He felt no pain at the time and, despite the shock of the cold water and the burning in eyes and throat from its coating of oil fuel, was aware only of a feeling of relief. He was a strong swimmer, confident now that he would survive.

His messmate, LSA Sims, a poor swimmer, had made for the picket boat, which was then still secured to the port boom forward. Sims ran out along the boom and dropped into her just as she was cut loose, her bows already rising out of the water.

It was Wilson who had given the order to cut. Coming out of the same galley as Sims and Batterbury, he had made for the port side, while most of the men with him melted away to starboard. He slid over the side between the two forward guns of the battery, then fell into black space. It was a long way down, a long drop in darkness before he hit the bilge keel, which was already clear of the water. In the tension of the moment he felt no pain, only a jolt. He still held his torch in his hand.

He clambered out of the water into the picket boat which, designed to take fifty-nine men, must now have had over 100 aboard, crammed into the forepeak, the cabin aft, and on deck, with other men, in the water, hold-on to her. So heavily was she laden that her sides, amid-ships, were almost awash. Wilson thought it was time to cut free. He was well-known, not for his rank, but because he was a popular turn at ship's concert parties. Men would recognise his voice as that of a 'Chiefy,' and obey. He and a Midshipman began shouting orders and, rocking under her terrible load, the bottom of the battleship coming up underneath her, the rope securing her to the boom parted. But there was no power to move her, although Leading Stoker Boyle was down in the engine room, trying to get steam up.

Wilson and the Midshipman shouted orders for some of the men to lie down in the gunwales and paddle at the water with their hands. Slowly, very slowly, the picket boat moved away from the heeling battleship. As she did so, a man came hurtling down the side of the *Royal Oak*, struck the rolling chocks (wooden stabilisers fitted to the underwater part of the hull), bounced off, fell into the water; and came swimming fast for the picket boat. It was Leading Seaman Boxall, released from his duty of trying to free the Carley raft. More and more men in the water began to head for the picket boat.

Up on 'B' gundeck. Commander Nichols and Chief Stoker Lawrence had in quick succession thrown a dozen or so 'church deals' down the side; at this moment, they had hold of another one. Lawrence recalls that there was now a final explosion, and that Nichols cried, 'Good God, this is ours, come on!' Holding the ends of the plank, they ran and slid down towards the water. It was a little late. Nichols found the guardrail somehow above him, scrambled over, tried to walk, not down the side, but up it – for the ship was rolling over – and was then 'quite gently' launched into the water. Lawrence, having dropped the 'church deal,' found water lapping at his feet, made a tremendous effort, and leapt out as far as he could. He went down into the water and recalls its phosphoresence; when he came up, he found that his right arm was useless and that he could not swim.

Bendell, too, remembers that final explosion and the great lurch of the ship which followed it. One moment, he had his feet in the sink of the pantry in the POs' mess, and was struggling to get out of the port. He could see the stars, but no land, through the port, for the land had now dropped below his level of vision. Then the whole compartment seemed to turn upside down, and he fell backwards into it in a shower of broken crockery; water poured in through the door, and a torrent came through the port. In a moment, he was was up to his chin in water. But there the water stayed, just allowing him to breathe. There was an 'airlock' in the flooded companment.

Just a moment or two before, Fossey and Harley, trapped in the signal house by the slamming of the door, had managed to tear away the 'light-excluding ventilator' on the starboard side; such was their desperation that Fossey nearly ripped off the top of one of his fingers. Harley, clad only in vest and pants, went through first, then helped Fossey who was fully dressed, with watchcoat and seaboots on. They stood for a moment at the top of the ladder, with the sea coming up to them, as the ship rolled over. 'Don't rush down. Stripy, stay where you are,' said Fossey, and took a last glance into the signal house to look at the clock. He thought it registered 1.27.

Then the ship gave a terrific lurch to starboard. Up till then Fossey had somehow been convinced that the *Royal Oak* was too big to sink. Now he realised that she was done. 'I think that was the first time I'd ever said my prayers, and meant it.' He went over quick from the sponson deck, hitting his leg on something. Then, with a damaged leg, a finger nearly torn off, and fully dressed with seaboots on, he swam for his life away from the *Royal Oak*, which was coming over on top of him.

CHAPTER SIX

'The Whole Works Went Up'

(AMIDSHIPS)

The main bulk of the *Royal Oak*, amidships, was taken up by engine and boiler rooms, together with the Central Stores. Aft, under the batteries, were two stokers' messdecks connected by a cross passage; forward of these were the Communications mess and the Boys' mess, on port and starboard sides respectively. Here, the first explosion in the bows had been vaguely heard and dimly felt. The second explosion occurred directly under the Boys' messdeck, from which there were hardly any survivors; the third was directly below the Stokers' mess; the last, after an interval, was aft again, under the Marines' messdeck.

Stoker Cleverley had got back into his hammock, just aft of the cross-passage. Above it was a perforated metal plate which carried the electric leads; Cleverley used it as a shelf for cigarettes and matches. He had almost got off to sleep again, when 'the whole works went up.' He was not backward in getting out of his hammock, but Leading Stoker Jones was faster still, perhaps because he was wide-awake after coming off duty. Jones covered the few feet between his hammock and the door in the after bulkhead. Outside there was a ladder which led up into the lobbies by 'X' barbette, from where it was possible to get out onto the quarterdeck. He was halfway up that ladder when the third explosion took place.

Cleverley, however, had only just jumped out of his hammock. As his feet hit the deck, it seemed to him that an explosion opened up the armoured deck in the cross-passage leading to the port-side Stokers' mess. The flash of it leapt out from there and struck men standing all around Cleverley; there was an appalling crash, and the lights went out.

Everything was black and red; everything burnable was smouldering, the hammocks glowing in the darkness. Cleverley, and about half-a-dozen other men, were on their feet; the rest of the stokers were huddled in the darkness where they had been thrown by the flash and blast. He could not understand why it was that they were dead or dying, and he still alive.

Unaware that the flash had burnt him from the knees downwards, he reached for the box of matches on the carrier lead, but found that the matches would not strike. Then he shinned up a ladder into the starboard battery and, in the pitch-darkness, lost himself.

Jones, already on the ladder at the third explosion, was shielded from the flash by the bulkhead; but, immediately afterwards, saw coming at him out of the dark from the direction of the Marines' messdeck aft, 'a massive ball of orange flame.' It was burning cordite, travelling in search of air too fast to run away from – he was in it for no more than a second, but instead of being on the ladder, he found himself flat on the deck. For some reason he did not then understand, he was unable to get up. When he did pull himself upright, the flame came travelling back, but this time did not throw him down.

He got up into the battery, turned to go forward, then heard, amid the crash of six-inch shells falling out of their racks with the heel of the ship, a shout of, 'Keep going aft – everybody aft!' After that, he too lost sense of direction and began blundering about in the darkness. Protected only by a thin vest, he had severe cordite burns on legs, shoulders, arms, head and face – and was unaware of it.

Most of the men awakened from sleep wore only singlet and shorts, apart from a wrist watch and a money belt. Only officers or petty officers normally wore pyjamas. In the portside Stokers' messdeck hammocks caught fire, and as the sleeping men fell through them, they too began to blaze. Chief Stoker Philip Terry, who had told them all to dress at the first explosion, tried to beat out the flames on one stoker, and was badly burned about the hands in doing so. Another, Stoker T..., clad only in blazing underwear, was dashing around, calling out terribly. The last seen of him was as he ran into the worst of the fire.

Terry and Stoker William Campbell then dashed onto the Boys' messdeck, where equally terrible sights met them. One of the Boys' instructors, probably Petty Officer Nicolls, was trying to organise an orderly evacuation of the messdeck. It seems probable, too, that it was Petty Officer French and Able Seaman Judge who were then trying to help boys through the manhole in the main hatch. So few boys survived that accounts are fragmentary.

Both Terry and Campbell got through into the starboard battery and then up another ladder onto the upper deck; Terry made for the big power launch, going out along the boom towards it. Stoker Albert Bond tried a different route and made the upper deck by the forward HA guns on the port side. All three had been badly burned.

Less than thirty boys escaped from the *Royal Oak* and most of these had been sleeping, not in the messdeck, but in the three forward casemates of the starboard battery directly above. Boy A W Scovell even went back for his trousers but, in the darkness, could not find them. He climbed up a ladder into the galley flat, with a mass of other boys; as they tried to open a door, water began to come through it, so they swarmed up another ladder onto the boat deck. For Boy G L Trewinnard the sinking of the *Royal Oak* was merely the first adventure in a long series when he was still very young – he was sunk in the following year off Norway, in the *Vandyke*, spent five years as a PoW and some time after that in Russia when the Red Army came. He hardly remembers how he got out of the *Royal Oak*, except that it was with his pal, Ernest Upham. Scovell remembered very well how he left, because he lost his footing on the boat deck – probably it was smothered in oil flung up by the explosions – and went straight into the drink.

This was directly by the starboard boom. The launch, ordered away by Commander Nichols just after the first explosion, was still secured to it. But, unlike the picket boat, which was being pulled out of the water, the launch was being forced under; the boat ropes were bar taut and the end of the boom was jamming the launch.

Scovell tried to get into it, but both he and the launch were by now too slippery with oil fuel; failing to get a grip, he slid back into the water. Men in the launch were trying to help swimmers on board and others were throwing out gratings for them to cling to. Chief Stoker Terry, both arms and hands badly burned, was struggling desperately to clear the boat and get it away to save life. Then Stoker Petty Officer Welch shouted to him,

'Get clear. Chief, she's coming over!'

Scovell had already gone, swimming away from the bridge and tripod which was heeling over above them; at the last moment, Terry dived overboard and struck away. The spotting top hung for a moment above them all then, as the ship rolled onto her starboard side, it fell in a sheet of spray, carrying the wreckage of the launch with it.

In the Communications messdeck, opposite the Boys' mess, the second and third explosions did not cause a fire. Leading Telegraphist Raymond Jones leapt out in his underwear, leaving a fortnight's pay behind, and, with half-a-dozen of his messmates and a crowd of others, probably stokers, swarmed up the ladder into the port battery above. The lights had gone, but they could see, dimly and intermittently, by the flashes as an electric cable short-circuited.

One last ladder led to the upper deck. There was quite a scramble around it. 'There was no panic or anything,' said Jones, 'it was just that there weren't many ways of getting up top. I suppose something like a thousand men had to funnel themselves onto the deck via about six gangways. It. takes time, particularly in the small hours, when everyone has been woken from a deep sleep. There was a certain amount of jostling.'

The final exit to the sea was through a heavy door in the narrow gallery which ran round the superstructure. Jones had a horrible feeling that he might not be able to open that door, but it was not secured and he emerged onto the upper deck, about ten yards from the port boom. The picket boat had already cast off, but he heard people shouting up around the gun turrets and saw figures silhouetted against the sky, apparently at work throwing Carley rafts over.

He had not stopped to think yet; but he did now, and decided – into the water, if possible. With the boom sticking up in the air at about 30°, he went over the guard-rails and slid down the side for about eight feet until he hit the boom platform. He carried on sliding, but was checked again by the narrow ledge at the top of the blister. 'So far,' said Jones, 'it was all paintwork – comfortably smooth sliding.' After that, he went on to seaweed and barnacles for quite a distance, until he hit the rolling strakes; the wooden blocks held him for a moment during which he looked beyond them and saw blackness – the surface of the water. He seemed to be sliding all the time, and never getting any nearer to it – which was partly true because, as he went down, the side was coming further and further out of the water, increasing the distance he had to travel.

From the rolling strakes downwards, he had no idea what happened to him; he just found himself below the surface, looking up through the water at the phosphorescent bubbles caused by his splash. Then he saw a Carley raft bobbing about, and made for it. His watch, which he still has, stopped finally and for good at 1.29.

Supply Petty Officer Finley had been standing, a deck above Jones, outside the mail office just under the bridge; he judged that the second explosion was directly opposite him. 'For me,' he said, 'this was my first real explosion. There was a dash, and I kicked my shoes off, because there'd be a swim for it.' He ran to the ladder which led up into the CPOs' and POs' Recreation Space, and had climbed it as far as the hatch combing when the third explosion seemed to hit directly below. It was the same explosion which had blown the armoured deck in the cross-passage and cut down the stokers.

'From then,' said Finley, 'as it hit, I was hit. All I can remember is a terrible flash and terrific heat.' He flung up his arms to protect his face and can remember falling.

He came to, lying under bits of broken wood, probably from the card tables in the Recreation Space. He could feel the ship gradually heeling over. He shoved the wood away and put a hand to his head. 'I found I'd no hair left and the flesh was hanging in strips from my arms. So something terrible had crashed me. I didn't worry about that, then – my sole intention was to get out as quick as I could.'

He saw another man there, and, in the dim light, linked hands with him. There was a stink of cordite, or something similar. Someone said, 'Strike a match.' The two men stumbled out into a cross-passage and went through another door into the Wardroom. As they stumbled down the slope of the deck, Finley lost the other man. He came to a door, looked out, saw the water – and a six-inch gun pointed down at an angle of 20° to 36°. Finley thought, 'Thank God!' and dived in.

Stoker Oswald Fletcher cannot have been far from Finley, for he was caught by the flash outside the Police office, then followed him up the ladder and into the Wardroom, burnt on his legs and face. By that time there were about thirty men trying to get out of the Wardroom, dashing round in the dark and being pinned and crushed by the furniture as it broke loose with the increasing heel of the ship. Fletcher was lucky, for his groping fingers found a 'light-excluding ventilator,' which he unscrewed and pulled out. When he climbed through the port, he found that the water was almost up to it.

Other men, pouring up from the Stokers' messdeck into the darkened after part of the battery – the forward part was on fire – had blundered into the lobbies under the Wardroom. Jones was in pitch-darkness until someone pulled aside the hessian blackout curtain obscuring the screen door onto the quarterdeck; the grey darkness of the night had a different quality, and he stumbled towards it. Once outside, he was walking in water, and must have passed quite close to where Paymaster Commander Cundall was lying helpless by the guardrails. Cleverley was stumbling about blind in what he knows now, but did not know then, was the Gunroom. But he felt cold air, and knew what that meant – a 'light-excluding ventilator.' 'I was in a bit of a panic, because the ship was on her beam ends, nearly.' He then performed the incredible feat of diving straight through the ventilator, taking it with him; he was in the water at once, for the quarterdeck was under. When he looked up, he saw 'X' turret above him. 'Then I broke all records for thirty yards, because the ship was coming over.'

Opposite these lobbies, on the port side of the ship, were the 'heads,' where the long queue had been assembled and, nearby, the Divisional office, where Petty Officers Kerr and Puddy had been standing. Both were knocked flat by the second explosion. The bulkheads moved and shook. Dommett, seeing to his horror an orange pillar of cordite flame come leaping up the hatch by the 'heads,' tried to outrun it. He was knocked flat on his face, but got to hands and knees in time to see the flame destroy the double curtains of the screen door and vanish out onto the quarterdeck, leaving behind blazing fragments which burnt him as he staggered after it. Quite dazed, he stumbled along the rails, well past where the *Daisy* was lying, the thought uppermost in his mind being that he had promised to tell his friends what had happened. Gradually, as the ship heeled over, he realised that he never would get back to the mess. He knew that his hair had been burnt off, but was not yet aware of any other injuries.

On the second or third explosion Instance, just buttoning up in the 'heads,' remarked to Able Seaman Hearn, 'We'll be going back to Pompey for a refit if this goes on!' Both turned away and made for the entrance. On that, there was a double bang aft, a blast of hot air, and a bright orange flame hit both men, hurling them back inside the 'heads.' For what seemed an eternity, the blazing cordite roared round and round the narrow space. The pain was excruciating.

Instance had put on thick trousers and a jersey, which protected his body; but there was no protection for his head and hands. He buried his face in his hands, then the pain at the back of his neck was so terrible that he clasped that instead. But the flame scorching at his face made him clap his hands over his eyes. To breathe was death. It was a question of how long he could endure the agony and still hold his breath.

Then the flame was gone. After that glare, the darkness was impenetrable. Instance found himself on hands and knees, unable to stand – why, he did not know. He began to pull himself forward and, just outside the door, crawled over the body of a man. The corpse was wearing only vest and pants – 'he must have gone up like a match,' said Instance.

He had no idea what had happened to Hearn and Hancock, who had been next to him in the queue; he next saw them, covered to the eyes in bandages, in hospital. 'All I knew was, that I was singed, and that I wanted fresh air; I wanted to get out.' He began to crawl in the pitch-darkness towards a cross-passage which would lead eventually to the starboard screen door. He knew there were hatches ahead of him, and that he might fall down them. He could see nothing whatever, he was guided only by his knowledge of the ship.

Meanwhile, Kerr and Puddy had picked themselves up, coughing violently from cordite gas in the lungs. By the Divisional office there was no fire yet, but the second explosion had blown down the hessian curtains 'at the officers' bathroom – and that was their escape route to a door which led into the port battery. 'Here you are, lads, in here!' called out Kerr.

After him dashed Puddy, Marine Sandford, and another man. he did not recognise in the dark. 'It wasn't dark for long,' Kerr said, in an account written shortly afterwards. 'Fire seemed to be eating the air and we were all coughing.' Sandford tried to open the door leading to the battery, then ran, shouting, 'We're done, it's stuck.' Sandford did find an alternative route, got over to the port side, and died there.

Kerr stuck to the door, but the list of the ship had wedged the handles inside the framework. Through the cracks in the door Kerr could see there was an inferno beyond, the handles were getting too hot to touch; but behind them there was no retreat, the fire was at their backs. In desperation Kerr, who is a big, heavy man, began to kick at the door. When it seemed he must suffocate with the fumes, it gave, and Kerr shouted, 'Come on, lads, it's opened!'

But there was no sign of anyone near him now, there were only sounds. Men were coughing and somebody was running around in a bad way, calling out, 'Oh, oh!' And from somewhere in the starboard casemates there was a terrible screaming.

The worst was still ahead of him. He flinched back from the red flames outside, then forced himself to run deliberately into them. There was no other escape. For a moment, he staggered and nearly fell, his legs seeming to fold under him helplessly. Then he was through, blundering about and clutching out for support. He pulled himself along by a hammock, then fell over something. His hands caught hold of guard rails and a chain – and he knew then that he was at the hatch outside the 'heads.' The port side screen door was not far away.

As he made for it, an explosion came up the hatch he had just left – but it seemed to blow forward and miss him. There was nothing to stop him now, the cordite flame had dissolved the hessian curtains, and he could see where the 'black night' was. Minutes after Dommett, he made the quarterdeck, and the fresh air seemed to revive him.

Instance was still travelling on hands and knees through the darkened cross-passage inside the ship. When he came to a turning into the starboard screen passage, despite his dreadful injuries, he knew where he was. He had served before in this class of ship, and knew them blindfold; otherwise he never would have got out.

After pulling himself thirty feet along the screen passage, he came to the hessian curtain. Normally there would have been an armoured door, clipped down. Now there was only the curtain to drag aside. He pulled it back, and looked out onto the quarterdeck.

It was heeled over at an angle of 45°. He had not been crawling along the deck at all for that last thirty feet, but on the bulkhead. It was, too, the first indication he had that the ship was sinking.

Instance pulled himself up by the framework of the door, stepped out onto the quarterdeck – and felt his legs go from under him. He skidded down the deck, cracked open the right side of his head on some projection, and arrived in a heap at the starboard guardrails. Standing there, telescope under his arm, the water pouring onto the deck and up over his feet, was a Midshipman. It was probably the Midshipman of the watch. 'Do you think we should abandon ship?' said the boy.

As he spoke, the battleship lurched heavily, the guard-rails went right under, and they both floated off into the icy sea.

CHAPTER SEVEN

'BEGGAR THIS FOR CIVVY STREET'

(AFT)

The Marines' messdeck lay around the barbette of 'Y' turret, separating the crew's quarters from the officers' cabin flat; it stretched right across the ship, with the barbette roughly in the centre. Directly above was the quarter-deck. Right forward of the mess, in a cross-passage, was a ladder at the top of which was a sliding armoured shield. To starboard, forward, there was a way out which led into the battery on that side. Aft, there were heavy water-tight doors in the bulkhead, one port and one starboard, which led into the cabin flat and so to a ladder to the quarter-deck.

At 1.16 the messdeck was an orderly array of mess-tables and hammocks, with most of the men turned in. A moment later, it was a blazing shambles.

Sergeant Parham, the gunnery instructor, was just finishing his cigarette. Near him some Marines were standing by the hammock netting. He heard two explosions and saw a flame go in among the Marines, cutting them all down. He himself was only 'singed,' so he ran into the messdeck and tried to wake people who were seemingly still asleep in their hammocks. He shook Corporal E W Cunningham, who did not stir, then ran to the water-tight door leading to the cabin flat on the port side. He began to knock off the clips, to open it, but was hampered by a crowd of about twenty men, all trying to get at it; the last clip on the left would not move because people were already pulling at the door. By now the whole messdeck was shuddering – probably it was the shaking of the ship as enormous masses of water boiled into her engine rooms and poured onto the decks as the 'light-excluding ventilators' slowly went under with the increasing heel; Parham thought it meant she was going any moment.

Saltmarsh's hammock had collapsed, and he went sprawling on the deck by the barbette. Barry Hawes found his hammock on fire, and leapt out. Stanley Rowlands ran for the way out into the starboard battery, found sounds of pandemonium coming from there – and the door jammed. He wasted no time at it – 'you only had seconds in which to operate' – but ran back to the mess-deck.

Sergeant Booth, looking forward, saw a flame come along the port lower passage – and fell back out of the way. 'The next thing I remember is seeing hammocks ablaze, messtables burning, and crockery falling off them – a cup on the deck was rolling backwards and forwards. I remember thinking, "Who knocked the handle off that cup?" I got to my feet and wondered why I was slipping – then I realised the ship was listing. As the flame hit one man, I saw a look of intense fright and pain come onto his face, then the flesh just curled off, like paper off a wall. There was a sudden smell, of pork cooking and burning wool. As he fell towards me, I gripped him by the arm – a piece of flesh came off, showing bone underneath. He fell on the deck a yard away from me, moaning. Everyone seemed to be shouting and screaming. Men were on their hands and knees, calling out for their mothers, in the knowledge they were mortally wounded. Others were crying in agony, "F...g roll on!" Flesh was hanging off some of them.'

On the starboard side, men were falling in flames out of their hammocks, and seeming to fall into flames, as if the deck below the hammocks had collapsed. The whole starboard side of the messdeck seemed to be melting and caving in. Barry Hawes, leaping from his burning hammock, dodged round it, and saw that the starboard water-tight door, aft, unlike the port door, was slightly ajar. He ran straight through in his underwear and into the Officers' quarters, and did not see what happened after that. Marine Owens was through it on his heels, with the cries of burning men in his ears; he does not want to remember.

Sergeant Booth saw a man's hammock burning, with the man lying silently in it; he ran his hands up it, to put out the flames. The man fell out, onto the deck, and lay there, dead, or past hope. Another man was jammed up in his hammock, with the cap box hooks driven into his body. When Booth tried to release him, he remained inert and silent.

When the third explosion occurred, some quarter of a minute or more after the second, a searing flash, coming from forward, went right round the messdeck and a huge belch of flame roared up apparently through the deck on the starboard side. At that moment Sergeant Parham, struggling to get the last clip off the water-tight door, finally succeeded. Men poured through it, flinging back the heavy steel door and pinning him against the bulkhead. The lights went out, and the mess was left in a glowing darkness, the flames obscured by the smoke.

So far, the NCOs had managed to keep some sort of order. Saltmarsh, who was very young at the time, recalled one older man, experienced in world war one, to whom they all looked up. He forgot the name, but can remember him shouting orders in succession, to cope with each factor, until the situation went finally beyond all human control. When the first flame swept in, he had shouted, 'Come on, get those hoses reeled off!' Saltmarsh had run to obey. Then, when it was clear the fire could not be fought, he ordered him to open the portside water-tight door, which had now slammed shut. 'This voice,' said Saltmarsh afterwards, 'this one man, instilling sense into men just standing there, gawking. He was slapping 'em, chivving 'em, goading 'em on.'

It was probably Sergeant McLaverty, a first world war man, who did admit to forcibly getting Priestley, the 15-year-old bugler, out of his hammock, slapping him round the ears, and telling him to get on deck. In the reeking chaos of the heeling messdeck, dimly seen, other NCOs were giving up their own chances of escape. Corporal H D Jordan, an enthusiastic Rover Scout, kept a way open for other men to get through. Saltmarsh saw him, and thought it was a hatch he was holding open; McLaverty's recollection is that it was a water-tight door. At the last, he told Jordan to look after himself, and Jordan replied, 'No, Sergeant Mac, not till they're through.' But he was dead before that, shrivelled by the flames. Corporal Marsh died in the same way, in the boat-hoist that, hands over his face to protect them from the flames, as he saw the younger Marines through.

'Cats' Cunningham was the Corporal of Saltmarsh's mess. Noted for his scruffiness, he would stand up to the Colour Sergeant on behalf of a Marine, if he thought the latter was in the right. In Saltmarsh's opinion, he was worth 'two and a half ordinary Corporals.' Saltmarsh was suddenly called away from trying to open the water-tight door by a shout from Marine Tuckwood, 'Give a hand over here!' With Jimmy Woods, he ran over, to find Tuckwood supporting Cunningham, dreadfully burned about the head. At that moment the fourth explosion occurred, almost under the starboard side of the messdeck, where they were, and the whole pattern, of one man helping another, disintegrated.

Previously, the deck covering may have been on fire, giving the impression that the deck had itself collapsed; after this explosion, there was no further doubt about it. Stanley Rowlands, who had just doubled back from his fruitless attempt to get out into the battery, hung there appalled. His way aft was blocked by an enormous hole in the plating, belching smoke and flame. The ship lurched heavily, and Saltmarsh, losing his footing, fell down the incline towards the flaming gap. Other men. too, were rolling down towards it, then vanishing into the fires below. As Saltmarsh slid helplessly, he hit an obstruction – the combing of a small hatch leading below to the fan space – and there he hung for a moment.

At that instant, Sergeant Booth had been going up the ladder forward of the barbette, on the heels of two Marines. He had been helping men to get up through the sliding armoured hatch above, but had now judged it was time he looked after himself. The explosion and the lurch which followed unleashed the sliding armoured shield. Like a crude guillotine it slid easily on its runners, as it was designed to do; with massive power it slammed across the gap and caught the two nearly naked men squarely at the waist. What was left, the bloody lower halves of two bodies, fell back down the ladder on to Booth; and the three of them, the two half corpses and the one live man, thudded to the heeling deck.

As he hit. Booth grasped at the chain around the bottom of the ladder and hung on, to stop himself from sliding down the deck towards the starboard side. 'Down there,' he said, 'it didn't look like a messdeck anymore – there were fountains of water coming in – I couldn't understand how it got there – there were no tables visible, just oil – I could smell that – with things floating on it and flames blazing. And I thought, "Now, how am I going to get out?" '

Rowlands, right over on the starboard side, with the door to the battery jammed behind him and the deck opened up ahead, paused for a moment. 'The whole of the starboard messdeck had gone,' he said, 'I think the bowels were out of the ship. And water was absolutely pouring into her.'

The water must already have been lapping over the quarter-deck above him, it was forcing its way through the 'light-excluding ventilators' in a torrent.

'I couldn't describe it,' he said. 'Where hammocks had been, there wasn't anything. I saw a couple of Marines in flames – I didn't know if they were dead yet – they were lying at the far end of the messdeck. I got aft by crawling along where the deck is reinforced to the bulkhead. 'With his shoulder pressed to the side of the ship and his feet on that narrow ledge above the gap, he inched his way along towards the after water-tight door.

On the opposite side, Booth also was going aft, holding on to stop himself sliding. Saltmarsh was climbing up the deck on hands and knees, away from the inferno on the starboard side. Reaching the port side and using a messtable as a bench, he tried to open a port. Another man, he thought it was Marine Ellis, came to help him undo the cleats of the deadlight. When they freed it, 'it came down with a terrific whack and knocked somebody else off his hold. I didn't wait on that, but climbed through the porthole and sat down on the side of the ship.' The man Saltmarsh thought was Ellis came through after him, then said sharply, 'I'm going back for me money,' and disappeared.

Sergeant McLaverty, giving no thought to his German Mae West, got out by going forward under the port battery, where for a moment he saw Marine F W C Sandford. Sandford had been in the Officers' bathroom with Petty Officer Kerr, but had left when he found the door to the port battery jammed. He must have found an alternative route, for he was now coming towards McLaverty, shouting, 'Beggar this for civvy street!' Beneath him, the deck seemed to be buckling, and he vanished in the smoke. McLaverty found a ladder forward and went up it, 'in a blast of hot air, I didn't get my feet on the rungs.' Once on the quarter-deck, he had to put his foot on 'X' barbette to get enough push to reach the guard-rails.

Below, from the ruined messdeck, the first rush of Marines had already poured aft into the Officers' cabin flat. One of their officers, Lieutenant Benton, slept on the starboard side a few feet from the water-tight door. When the second explosion occurred, he stopped listening for aeroplanes, leapt out of his bunk, and made straight for the door, in order to find out what was happening on the messdeck. Then there was a third explosion and a red glow coming at him; the water-tight door slammed in his face, and the flame never reached him. He turned and ran aft, where he met the Dentist, Surgeon Lieutenant Dickie, the officer who had taken a third light from Keen's match. Benton was in pyjamas, Dickie in messkit. Rather white-faced, they asked each other what had happened. Then ten Marines, in various stages of undress, came running aft, and began to ask them the same question. There was a ladder nearby, leading to the quarter-deck, but it had a black hessian curtain around it. Perhaps they were subconsciously afraid of being caught in the curtain, but none of them made any attempt to get up it. The ship took on a noticeable list, the lights dimmed down and went out, and the fans ran down with a whining noise.

'This way!' yelled Benton, and ran for the only sliding door which was open; it led into the Admiral's pantry. He had to climb across a piece of furniture which had slid across the door, then jump down in bare feet onto a deck covered with broken crockery. He scrambled up onto the sink, beating about with his hands to find the port which he thought would be there. Then his hands, slapping steel, produced a hollow boom from a wooden 'light-excluding ventilator,' and he set to work on the butterfly nuts holding it in place. They were hard to move.

He was surprised that the men behind him were so patient, there were no cries of 'Hurry up!' It was so quiet that he could actually hear the water pouring in through the submerged 'light-excluding ventilators' on the starboard side. That made him hurry. The ventilator came away in his hands, and he slung it, wondering if he would be, after all that, too large a man to get through.

Barry Hawes, standing silent immediately behind him, was wondering exactly the same thing. 'I saw Benton's stern as he started to climb out – I wished he'd hurry up, and I wondered how long he'd take. Then, instead of diving into the sea, as I expected, he turned and crawled up on top. When I went through, I saw why – the ship was right over and you couldn't drop into the water, you'd have gone rolling down the port side.'

Owens, too, went straight past the ladder and on into the pantry, where he saw a Midshipman in pyjamas; he could also see grey sky through the port, and went right through it, followed by the Midshipman. Together they began to walk down the port side, the ship had heeled so much in that short time that it was now negotiable.

A rather hopeless little group were standing – or, rather, trying to keep their balance – in pitch darkness around the curtained ladder to the quarterdeck. Marine Moore, with one arm badly burned, had gone there after going through the port water-tight door opened by Parham. Rowlands was the last to arrive, having inched his way past the gaping inferno in the messdeck. After the glare of the flames, he could see nothing. Men were hammering at the hatch above, but even the manhole was battened down; in that darkness, they had little or no chance of opening it. 'It was very quiet,' said Rowlands, 'no one made much noise; you could hear the water coming in. I said my prayers.'

Then someone else arrived, there was a splutter of a match, and they could see what they were doing; in a moment, the manhole was opened and they poured onto the quarterdeck. They struggled forward to the gangway, holding onto the guardrails.

Below, Sergeant Booth was lying across a ladder. It should have been upright, but must by now have been nearly horizontal, he could feel it in his back. He could remember making his way aft as far as the water-tight door leading to the cabin flat. It had been blocked by a washdeck locker which had fallen over. He had got on top of that, then jumped. The list of the ship must have confused him, for he had struck his head violently on something. Now dazed, in pitch-darkness, he was beginning to feel frightened. 'Then,' he said, 'tremendous waves of noise beat in my ears – it was just as if I was tied to the clapper of a bell. And that's the last thing I remember of the *Royal Oak*.'

CHAPTER EIGHT

'Every Time a Coconut'

(QUARTER-DECK)

When the second explosion occurred followed, he thought, by two others in quick succession, Engineer Commander Renshaw was still superintending the opening of the capstan flat. The place filled immediately with dense smoke and the ship heeled over rapidly. There was obviously no chance of the Chief Stoker escaping from the trunk, the Captain had gone up the ladder to the forecastle, followed by the others, and Renshaw himself was nearly asphyxiated by the fumes. He, too, stumbled up onto the forecastle, where it was so dark that he could see nothing. Taking his torch out of his pocket, he made his way aft along the port side, his eyes gradually becoming accustomed to the gloom. As he came to 'B' turret, he could see men going over the boom into the picket boat;. it was obviously going to be overcrowded and, he thought, no place for him.

At this point, or very shortly afterwards, there was a great splash from the port side, as the spotting top carried away from the heeling tripod and fell into the sea. When Renshaw reached the quarter-deck he met Admiral Blagrove, who said, 'What caused those explosions, Engineer Commander?'

'Torpedoes, sir,' said Renshaw, who could think of no other cause.

'Good God!' replied Blagrove, in a tone of very great surprise.

The Admiral then went forward along the port side towards the bridge, the heel then being so great that Renshaw had to hold on to the guardrails. It seems certain that Batterbury was not mistaken when he recalled seeing the Admiral sitting on the guardrails near the bridge, calling out, 'Every man for himself,' or words to that effect. After that point, what happened to Admiral Blagrove seems to be hearsay, based on uncertain identifications in dim light.

A very short time only had elapsed since the second explosion, it may have been less than five minutes. On the starboard side, the launch had gone, apparently crushed by the spotting top; from the starboard scuppers, Cundall and Instance, lying burned, had floated off; when Jones and Cleverley followed them out of the screen door, the whole starboard side of the quarter-deck was already underwater.

Keen, Pirie, Owen and other junior officers were trying to unship the gig, right aft on the quarter-deck. Looking forward, Owen could see flames in the port battery and men coming out through them onto the quarter-deck. Kerr more or less fell through the screen door, the skin burnt completely away from his head and hands – he bears the 'tidemarks' of the inferno to this day. The fresh air revived him, and he went uphill to the guardrails and joined in an effort to get men down into the *Daisy II*. Contrary to what was generally believed by survivors, one man only stepped 'dry' into the drifter, and he was not an officer.

According to Skipper Gatt, this man seemed dazed and did not know how he had got there. Almost certainly it was Musician John Thompson, who afterwards told Kerr that he had been burned outside the 'heads,' and had gone straight down into the drifter from the quarter-deck. There were two reasons why no one else got into the *Daisy*, the first of them being that she was secured, not at the port accommodation ladder, but forward of it, leaving the gangway clear for boats to come alongside.

When the second explosion occurred. Skipper Gatt told the cook, the only other man on deck, to cut the head rope; he himself ran to the wheelhouse to ring for 'full astern.' The cook shouted out, 'I haven't got my knife!' so Gatt told him to throw the rope off the bollard. By then it was too late, the battleship's port blister, coming out of the water, was rising up underneath the *Daisy*, there was a dreadful grinding noise, and the drifter heeled over, tautening the head ropes so much that it was impossible to free them from the bollards. The battleship was then heeling one way with the drifter, caught on the blister, heeling the other; the stern of the *Daisy* was almost awash but her bows were twenty-five feet out of the water, locked by her bilges on to the *Royal Oak*'s blister. The grinding noises continued.

While this was happening Kerr saw a Midshipman and an officer, who, he thought, was Lieutenant-Commander Cook, trying to help men get down a rope into the heeling drifter; he himself went to another rope and, in spite of his burnt hands, helped men to climb down it. But the port side was rising out of the water and the drop was becoming longer every moment; the *Daisy* was heeling over, and the gap between her side and the quarter-deck was steadily increasing. With her engines at 'full astern,' in an effort to pull loose from the blister, water was frothing around the stern of the drifter; men were jumping from the quarter-deck, bouncing off the side of the battleship, and railing into this turmoil. There was a cry from the quarter-deck '*Daisy*, stop your engines!' An officer, standing on the quarter-deck, cast off her stern rope; it fell into the water, and wrapped itself round her screw.

An obvious way down to the water was by the accommodation ladder. Keen afterwards heard that Acting Lieutenant Vincent, the very junior Marine officer on duty, had marshelled an orderly file of men to go down it. As the ship listed, he stood there, shouting 'Roll, bowl, or pitch, every time a coconut, form queue here, my lucky lads!' But as the ship heeled over, the gangway rose higher and higher out of the water. Dommet, dazed from his burns, had been one of the first to go down it; from right down at the bottom of the ladder, he could see clearly what was happening. Men were jumping off all around him, but they were either hitting the battleship's port propeller shafts, now clear of the sea, or falling into the water boiling astern of the *Daisy*'s screw. He forced his way up the gangway, to try to stop any more men coming down the ladder and, with the aid of Surgeon Lieutenant E D Caldwell, succeeded. Then, with a roar, the *Daisy* slid off the blister, the head ropes having already parted with the strain, and Gatt immediately stopped his engine.

He handed a lifebuoy to a deckhand, but the man gave it back, saying 'No, you're a married man, I'm single.'

At this moment Benton, having got onto the quarter-deck from the Admiral's pantry, made his way with difficulty to the head of the accommodation ladder. Captain Edgar Balls, the senior Marine Officer, was by the guard-rails. Benton did not know then that he could not swim, but noticed only that he seemed very quiet. The *Daisy* had just gone astern out of it, and there were, Benton thought, at least thirty men left behind on the accommodation ladder, discussing the matter. 'Discussing,' said Benton, 'was perhaps not quite the right word for it, but no one had yet given any command to abandon ship and the majority verdict seemed to be, "Don't go yet – wait for the order".'

Then the hatch on the quarter-deck opened and a small group, Rowlands and Moore among them, burst out. Rowlands saw a Warrant Officer sitting down at the top of the accommodation ladder and crying like a child. Alarmed at the heel of the ship, he yelled, 'Come on, let's get out of it!' Engineer Commander Renshaw took off his shoes, went over the guardrails, and started to walk down the side. Able Seaman Farley, who had got out forward, was walking along the side towards the *Daisy*, hoping to get into her. Saltmarsh was sitting on the side, wondering what to do. There was an explosion, somewhere under the quarter-deck, and the ship gave a sudden lurch. Lieutenant Keen, heaving away at the starboard side of the gig, lost his balance, slipped, and went skidding down the deck into the sea. The gig came free, slid across the deck, and jammed up against a ventilator. 'At this point,' said Cadet Owen, 'I thought that was enough of that, and I went through the port guardrails.'

Midshipman Pirie thought the same, and jumped outwards from the stern; so did Lieutenant Henry Duncan and Barry Hawes, who just cleared the blister. Men were jumping and sliding down the port side, as it rolled up under their feet, tearing themselves open on the razor-like barnacles. Benton found it easy; the barnacles gave a grip to his bare feet. Keeping his balance, he ran down the side, saw a propeller shaft in front of him, thought, 'Shall I go over or under?' – and took a leap clean over it. Lieutenant Sclater slid under the shaft, cutting himself badly on the barnacles.

Dommett was hanging on to the port guardrails, watching 'X' and 'Y' turrets cast loose. Of their own accord, the guns slowly swung round and pointed their muzzles down at the water. Instance, swimming along the starboard side of the quarter-deck and still dazed by his burns, saw two fifteen-inch gun muzzles looking down at him, and thought it might be an hallucination.

At the lurch, the men holding on to ropes on the port side let go their hold; Kerr dropped the end of his rope and got outboard of the guardrails, which were now horizontal. Then he took off his jacket and trousers and laid them across the rails, thinking as he did so of the current silly-song, 'Hanging Up the Washing on the Siegfried Line.' He also mentally noted that he was going to lose the 14s in silver in the trousers pockets, then got hold of the fender rope, to prevent himself from slipping. When he got into the sea, he kicked off so violently that he sprained his foot. A few yards away, Parham did the same thing with a wire holding the accommodation ladder. Rowlands never made the port guardrails at all, he went sliding backwards across the quarter-deck into the sea.

The ship gave another lurch, as still more bulkheads gave way, and like a great whale, she rolled right over and stood on her fighting top. Engineer Commander Renshaw, having taken two steps down the side, was thrown over backwards into the sea. At that moment, Able Seaman Farley, running along the side towards where Renshaw was, was also thrown backwards over the quarter-deck. As he fell through the air, he had visions of hitting a turret or ventilator and suffering broken bones which, in the circumstances, would be the undoubted end of him. But nothing interrupted his fall, and he went down deep into water black with oil.

Five or six men came swimming away in a ragged line from the port side, singing, 'Roll Out the Barrel'; among them were Batterbury and a Marine, a senior NCO, with a greatcoat on. As he began to weaken, there were shouts of, 'Hang on, Stripey.' From the stern another group, in which was Barry Hawes, plunged in and struck out, singing like mad, 'Run, Rabbit, Run,' so pleased were they to have escaped. It was involuntary and quite spontaneous. Few looked back, they were all too intent on getting away from her, for fear of suction or an explosion in the magazines.

But leading Stoker Jones, well clear on her starboard side, saw a man running along the hull towards the stern; and Sims, who had been thrown off the picket boat, saw an explosion aft as she began the final lurch. Instance, close under her starboard side, and making away diagonally towards the stern, saw the ship in the dim light falling over towards him, and was conscious of the boats and gear which might carry away. 'The thing which struck me most,' he said, 'was the tremendous noise; it was like a huge tin, full of nuts and bolts, slowly turning over. Racks of shells must have been coming loose, and other gear, so that anybody still inside had no hope. It must have been an absolute nightmare.' Midshipman Pirie, holding on to a piece of wood astern of the battleship, saw her port propeller shafts clear of the water, then he saw her rudder appear and finally, as she rolled right over, one of her starboard screws. Inside her still were nearly 800 men.

Sergeant Booth never knew how he got out. His last memory was of lying across a ladder and then of a tremendous ringing noise in his ears. He came to, in the water, stark naked and clutching the cigarette lighter which his wife had sent him the previous day. It seems he can only have been blown out of the ship by that final explosion, which may have been a small-calibre magazine detonating.

Sick Berth Attendant Bendell was equally confused. One moment he had been attempting to get through the port-hole in the pantry of the Petty Officers' mess, then 'there was another bang, everything seemed to go upside down, and I fell back into the compartment. There was a clatter as pots and pans tell, too, and at the same time water came in at the port. Then, perhaps because the door had closed with the increasing heel of the ship, a bubble of air was trapped in the pantry. I don't really know what happened, or how it happened, but I had my head in air. Not much of it, I was touching the deckhead with my head. I think water had come in through the porthole, and that the ship was either on the bottom or completely upside down, with the starboard upper portholes submerged.' It was not the deckhead, but the deck, which he was touching with his head, for the ship was capsized; the air-lock must have formed on one side of the compartment, because the *Royal Oak*'s starboard side was nearer the seabed than the port side. The only exit now was the open porthole, some five feet down through the dark, oil-smeared water.

The surface of Scapa Flow was some forty or fifty feet above him, and the bottom of the *Royal Oak* was still visible. At least half-a-dozen men were still on the capsized hull. Marine Moore was one of them. Two of the boys, Trewinnard and Upham, were there; Trewinnard was taking his trousers off, in anticipation of a swim. The Navigator, Lieutenant-Commander Gregory, was walking up and down with a stoker, smoking. One of them had a packet of cigarettes, the other a box of matches, so they had lit up. Gregory was determined not to leave one minute before it was absolutely necessary. He did not fancy his chances in the bitterly cold water, and each minute spent out of it was one minute more of life. When Gregory felt it was time at last to go, he threw down his cigarette – and automatically made to stamp it out; then, with the stoker, he waded off the hull into the water, as if from a beach.

Fifty feet down, in the flooded compartment, Bendell had gone underwater and was fumbling around as if blindfolded for the porthole. He failed, and surfaced in the air-lock, gasping for breath. Then he took another gulp of air and went down again. He beat about frantically, but could not find the port, so floundered up towards the air-lock. It wasn't there. Either it had gone, or he had lost his sense of direction. 'Now I've had it,' he thought, and took a few mouthfuls of water, to end it quick.

The water must have been contaminated with oil fuel, for it made him sick. Writhing, he spat it out. Then, with no memory of finding the porthole, or even of going through it, he was shooting up towards the surface; lucky for him that he had exhausted the air in his lungs, or they might have burst when he reached the surface.

All that was left of the battleship now was a dark hump on the black water; from the swaying, laden picket boat, Chief E R A Wilson thought it looked like a football pitch, with froth bubbling around the sides. Leading Seaman Boxall, also from the picket boat, saw flickering lights from bow to stern, as if she was a furnace inside and some of the plates had started; Leading Seaman Instance, from the opposite side of the wreck, saw blue flashes, as if generators were being earthed; Supply Petty Officer Finley saw them, too. Marine Hawes thought she looked like a big whale. To Skipper Gatt, nursing the leaking *Daisy II*, she was a menace, a submerged obstruction beneath the oil-smeared water.

Slowly she went from sight, carrying down 800 living men, until her mainmast and fighting top struck the sea-bed and the whole 29,000 tons of her forced them like spears into the sand; she settled slightly on her starboard side, the muzzles of the fifteen-inch guns being forced up to full elevation. Gatt knew she could not be far down and that low water would probably reveal her. From the sunken hull, oil poured up in an endless stream, fouling the water in great, spreading waves many feet thick. And from somewhere near the sunken bow. Sick Berth Attendant Bendell scraped up the port side and broke surface, the last man alive out of the *Royal Oak*.

CHAPTER NINE

'DAISY, DAISY, GIVE ME YOUR ANSWER, DO'

On the water now were only two boats, the picket boat, which had no power, and the *Daisy*, with a rope wrapped round her screw. The liberty launch, tied to the starboard boom, and capable of holding hundreds of men, had gone – shattered by the spotting top as the battleship rolled over. The gig, with the cover still on it, had floated off the quarter-deck and was now drifting astern, water-logged. There was one Carley raft complete – just one – and buckled parts of other Carley rafts, probably those damaged in the gale and stacked on the forecastle. There were a number of 'church deals,' including those thrown down the side by Commander Nichols and Chief Stoker Lawrence; there were gratings thrown out from the launch; and the crew of the drifter were now throwing overboard anything that would float – lifebelts, gratings, bits of wood.

The water temperature was 48° F. In theory, the extreme limit of life for a man in the water, or floating in a Carley raft in contact with the water, would be two hours; but an hour would be more reasonable.[1] Out of the water, there was a biting wind which would kill just as quickly. Additionally, many of the swimmers were badly burned or bleeding from barnacle cuts.

[1] Based on table compiled by the USN after the war, to prove the ineffectiveness of the Carley raft, which has now been replaced in the Royal Navy by the self-inflating life raft with 'Arctic tent'; the raft, in its container, can be carried to the ship's side by two men. If the container goes down with the ship, the raft breaks free and comes to the surface.

The nearest land was half a mile away, it consisted of rocks backed by high cliffs; the nearest road was two-thirds of a mile inland from the cliffs, and there were hardly any dwellings, merely a few farmhouses. The Flow was utterly dark, no one saw any Northern Lights; nothing stirred and no alarm was given. Skipper Gatt began to signal 'SOS, SOS, SOS, SOS, SOS,' on the drifter's whistle, but there was no reaction. The main fleet anchorage was empty and the ships off Lyness, hidden behind the islands, heard and saw nothing. The nearest ship, from which help might come, was the old seaplane tender *Pegasus*, lying invisible in the gloom nearly two miles away to the west. She remained darkened and silent; she had seen nothing, she had heard nothing.

Even on the quarter-deck of the *Royal Oak*, almost on top of the explosions, they had seemed curiously vague and muffled; only a few men claimed to have seen any kind of flash and then, only one; one man only thought he had seen a pillar of water, and then from one explosion only. The cordite flame, when it escaped from the ship, must have been briefly visible, but only to someone looking right at it at the time; the fires raging inside the hull would not have been visible at all outside it.

Ernest Wheeler, a Gosport man, deckhand in the Admiralty waterboat *Fountain* lying at that moment tied to Lyness stone jetty, slept on, unaware that hundreds of his fellow townsmen were dead or dying at the other end of the Flow. Police Constable David Allan, on duty in the streets of Kirkwall, thought it would be a night just like any other; he had a friend in the *Royal Oak*, but did not suspect that he was then swimming for his life in the black water some three or four miles away. Afterwards, a well-known Orcadian recalled that it must have been that night he had been out walking with his cousin and that they had commented on the brilliance of the 'Merry Dancers' – the Northern Lights – and that they had begun to recite from memory Aytoun's lines,

> 'Fearful lights that never beckon
> Save when kings and heroes die.'

But this must have been before midnight, because the survivors recall only an ordinary starlit night, with no moon. Commander Nichols did think he saw Northern Lights about the time of the first explosion, but will go only as far as 'a fair aurora.' The men in the water could see the nearest cliffs, half-a-mile away, because they were silhouetted, but that was all; at first, they could not even see the *Daisy*, nor could they see other swimmers, unless their heads were very close.

There were no searchlights sweeping the Flow, no signal lamps flashing, no destroyers hunting for a submarine, and no depth-charges exploding. There were only bursts of singing from little groups of men in the water, and screams and cries from others, with 'SOS, SOS, SOS' hooting from the *Daisy*'s whistle. After a little while, two lights came on.

As the *Daisy* backed away from the sinking battleship, men in the water were already clinging to the seven motor car tyres tied to her sides as fenders. Hearn was hanging on to one, and four or five other men were holding on to him; he was in pain from his burns, but did not let go his hold. One man only was aboard from the battleship, staggering about dazed. Gatt and his crew began to haul out of the water the men clinging to the starboard side – there were at least twenty of them. The *Royal Oak* had already gone from sight, it had taken about seven minutes, thought Gatt. Then, while his crew threw out pieces of wood, he lifted a hatch to see what damage the drifter had sustained in sliding off the battleship's blister. It was in fact considerable, but she was not leaking very much, so Gatt assumed she was all right for the moment. But the swimmers in the water were spread out over many hundreds of yards; most of them could not see where the *Daisy* was, or even if she was still afloat; still less could anyone in the *Daisy* see them.

The drifter's funnel was painted white, so Gatt lit a gas lamp at the front of the wheelhouse and another on top, and this, shining on the funnel, was visible at least for several hundred yards. He thought that to show any more light would be imprudent; he did not know what had sunk the *Royal Oak*. Nor did anyone else. Some of the men in the water saw the lights at once, and to the ragged choruses of 'Roll Out the Barrel' and 'South of the Border' was, now added a third melody, 'Daisy, Daisy, Give Me Your Answer, Do.'

Very close to the *Daisy* were two groups of men, visible from her deck. The mate called out, 'Hard a port!' and Gatt, in the wheelhouse, obeyed; then he turned to starboard, to pick up the second group; and after that, seeing no more, lay stopped, waiting for the men somewhere in the outer darkness to swim to him. He knew they were there, he could hear them calling; and he shouted back, 'Swim towards us, we'll do our best.'

Benton, who was picked up almost immediately, while the *Daisy* was still moving, heard the drifter before he saw her; from the sound of her screw thrashing the water, he thought he was going to be run down, then realised that here was a means of saving himself. He grabbed for one of the rubber tyres, missed it, missed the next one, and caught hold of the last, to which other men were already clinging. When they started shouting, a deckhand looked over the side, got another man to help him, and began to haul the swimmers aboard.

He found himself in the boiler room, with about twenty others, all of them merely wet. They all took off their clothes, wrung them out, then put them on again. 'Then,' said Benton, 'the oily ones started coming in, and in very gentlemanly style we made room for them in the warm part; eventually, down came those who'd been burnt. Skin was hanging in shreds down their arms, there was a lost look in their eyes – they were staring, with mouths half open, saying, 'Don't touch me, don't touch me.' The flesh had slipped down their arms like a woman's gauntlet, folded sometimes over the hands – perhaps that happened when men had to grab hold in order to pull them inboard.'

One of the first of these lost creatures was Ordnance Artificer Dommett. He had swum away from the ship when she was upside down, with a feeling of irritation all over his body; it was the burnt fragments of pyjamas rubbing on his seared flesh. He freed himself from these charred remains, saw the light appear on the *Daisy*, and headed towards it, tearful that she would move away. His cries were answered by voices telling him to plod on, there were many more swimmers coming on behind him. 'Then,' said Dommett, 'in that dark night, with only the reflection of the *Daisy*'s light on the water as relief, I became conscious of a darker wave rolling up towards me and as it swept over and passed me I knew I was in a sea of oil.'

When that wave passed on, the white faces and arms of the unburnt swimmers became black, making them virtually invisible in the darkness.

'After what appeared an age I reached the starboard quarter of the drifter and two fellows held a pole over the side for me to climb up. It was only then I realised I was in a bad way. As I held up my hands to grasp the pole, they gasped, 'That poor devil can't climb – look at his hands.' Still, with their efforts I got aboard, naked except for my liberal coating of oil fuel. The lads led me just as I was down below and put me in one of their bunks. I often wonder and hope they were issued with new kit and thanked.'

Some of the uninjured survivors now began to help with the hard work of getting slippery, oil-covered swimmers out of the water; others helped them below, first to the boiler room, then the crews' cabin, and finally, to the fish hold, as more and more men had to be crammed into the drifter. Some officer survivors, including Lieutenant Duncan, helped supervise the rescue work, while a Lieutenant-Commander took over at the whistle, continually sending out 'SOS,' without any apparent effect. Other survivors, including Batterbury, went back into the water time and again to help out men too far gone to help themselves.

Batterbury also had been overtaken by the oil, as he swam away with half-a-dozen other men in a ragged line from the port side. He felt as though he were swimming completely in oil, not in water at all, and his movements became sluggish, although he was a strong swimmer. It was too much for the Marine NCO, labouring along in his greatcoat. He called, 'Cheerio, fellers, I can't hang on' – and was gone.

There was a Carley raft nearby, but it was well loaded, so he made for the cover of a fishhatch, probably thrown out from the *Daisy*, on which a man was lying unconscious. All this took place in a matter of minutes, because the belly of the *Royal Oak* was still visible, with men moving about on it, and almost immediately the *Daisy* came by and Batterbury climbed up a rope into her. After that, the *Daisy* lay stopped, moving only in response to shouts from out of the darkness. Then by now oil-blackened faces of the swimmers made a visual search impossible; there was also the danger of ramming the submerged hull of the wreck and further opening the *Daisy*'s plates. It was a great strain on Skipper Gatt who, from the wheelhouse, could see very little.

Before the ship had even disappeared Instance, swimming weakly away from the stern, heard a voice calling him from out of the darkness. It was, he thought, his Divisional officer. Lieutenant A H Terry, clinging to a piece of wood. 'Who are you?' called the voice.

He shouted back, 'I'm Instance, and I'm burned to beggary.'

'Hard luck, old man,' came the reply, 'but we'll be all right here.'

After five or ten minutes of hanging on to the wood, they saw a light, which was the *Daisy*, and the officer suggested swimming to it. Instance willingly agreed, but at once found he could not keep up; after a few strokes he stopped, floundered around, swallowed some water – which turned out to be oil – and could no longer see the officer, who had disappeared ahead in the gloom. But he was not going to drown now, and somehow kept afloat for what may have been half-an-hour, until he heard another voice calling him in the darkness. Someone said, 'Hang on, we're coming,' and a small raft appeared, paddled by three men, one of whom

Full helm: Royal Oak *on exercises. First World War.*

The Iron Duke, *Admiral Jellicoe's flagship at Jutland and since used as training and depot ship. She was anchored ten miles from where the* Royal Oak *was sunk. Badly damaged in an air attack, she was subsequently beached.*

Royal Oak *firing a broadside.*

HMS Royal Oak, *on the way to Skapa Flow, 1939.*

HMS Repulse *hit amidships.*

Chief ERA C J Wilson. A torch bought the previous day played a big part in his escape.

AB A J Farley who was hurled into the air as the Royal Oak *turned completely over.*

The Repulse *in the North Atlantic. Unmodernised and a battle-cruiser she was the weakest of the big ships – although one of the fastest.*

The Germans claimed that what Prien had taken to be Repulse *was in fact the 6,900-ton* Pegasus, *bought by the Royal Navy in 1914 as a seaplane carrier and until the 1930s known as* Ark Royal.

The starboard gangway to the quarter-deck and the forward boom with boats secured. On the night of the sinking, the drifter Daisy II *was tied up forward of the port gangway and, the boats having been destroyed or sunk, was responsible for the saving of 386 lives.*

Commander Prien in his conning-tower of U-47.

U-47 heading for it's target.

U-47, returning after the sinking of the Royal Oak *arrives at Kiel, Germany, on 23 October 1939, with her crew at quarters. The battleship* Scharnhorst *is in the background.*

Prien's claims – only much later could they be put to the test – seized the imagination of the world. On his safe arrival back he received congratulations. This was but a prelude to the honours to come. The Führer himself sent for the crew, congratulated each man personally and decorated Prien with the Knights Cross (below).

was Shipwright Warrant Officer Harding. The raft was probably only half a raft, and the paddle was merely a piece of driftwood.

Someone caught hold of his hands and tried to pull him up onto the raft. Instance screamed in agony. He did not know until that moment just how badly he had been burned. Someone else called, 'Pull him up by his hair.' But he had no hair. Eventually they got a grip under his arm pits and hauled him in that way. Instance sat there, so grateful for his rescue that he tried to help paddle by using his hands; then he passed out.

Around the sunken bow, several Carley rafts were bobbing about in the water; one of them complete and undamaged. Leading Telegraphist Jones, after skidding down the side, surfaced to find this one only a few feet away from him, so some devoted group must have managed to get it away before the battleship turned over. A moment or so later Commander Nichols, who had only abandoned ship when she gave her final lurch, joined him on the raft. Shortly afterwards. Chief Stoker Terry arrived and soon the raft was so heavily loaded with men that it sank beneath them; Jones, who is a tall man, found himself up to his chest in water, but still standing on the raft. Some of the men then got off, and as it rose to the surface again, hung on to the sides.

Struggling in the water nearby, hampered by watchcoat and seaboots, was Leading Signalman Fossey. From another buckled raft the two boys, Trewinnard and Upham, heard him splashing and shouting in a dazed fashion, 'Is there any boats?' They managed to pull him to their raft, which was of use only to cling to, then saw the other complete raft a short distance away. A man shouted to them that it was too full, but as Fossey was injured, they ignored that and Jones put out a hand and hauled Fossey to safety. Chief Stoker Lawrence, who had gone in at the same time and place as Commander Nichols, also owed his life to a friend. Unable to swim, because he had injured his right arm in going over, he remembers hooking his left arm round a plank. Chief Mechanician Kim also had hold of the plank, and, unknown to Lawrence, held on to him for forty-five minutes until they were found by the *Daisy*.

Captain Benn must have found the buckled raft, or another like it, because he was reported to have said afterwards that he had thought he was doing well until he saw Commander Nichols go past him on his 'Rolls Royce.' In point of fact the Carley raft is not adapted to progression and this one was going round in circles. It was certainly doing so when, after what seemed to him a long time, Blundell reached it. He was on his way to the shore and nearly done; he had taken off his wrist watch, because he thought the tiny weight might make just that bit of difference, but he hung on to his belt with the £13 1s. in it. A strong swimmer, he had not reckoned on the oil, which seemed a foot thick at least. At the raft, they made room for him to hang on to the side, one injured man growling, 'Mind my bloody arm.'

To help propel the raft, he began kicking out with his legs. There were no paddles, and people on the raft were using their hands. When they saw the lights of the *Daisy* come on. there were shouts of, 'Make for that light.' Other men, however, thought the shore was nearer, and paddled in that direction. The raft lurched along in circles; but the effort kept them warm and some began singing. Fossey, lying on it, with a finger almost torn off and one leg completely numb, dimly remembers 'South of the Border' and the inevitable 'Roll Out the Barrel.'

It was deathly quiet all around them now, partly because they were moving away towards the cliffs and partly because the shouting and screaming in the water had ceased. There was an ominous reason for that.

When Sims had swarmed down into the picket boat, she had cast off but, having no steam up, had remained rocking in the water beside the heeling battleship until Wilson and one or two others had got men to lie down by the gunwales and paddle with their hands. Then, already overloaded, she proved a magnet for every man swimming near her; Boxall reached her before the *Royal Oak* sank, and got on deck, which was packed with men, sitting and standing. The forepeak, engine room, and after cabin were crammed with men and her sides were nearly awash. Kerr, badly burned, swam to her but found the sides jammed with men hanging on and threshing the water; he got a grip, but the men on either side of him seemed in a very bad way, so he back-stroked clear to give them more room. She was swaying dangerously, but someone in her started up with 'South of the Border, Down Mexico Way' and those in the water joined in.

Suddenly the singing stopped, as another rush of swimmers came away from the battleship and made for the picket boat, which was heeling over to starboard. Wilson heard someone shout, 'Trim the dish,' in an attempt to right her, and saw men obediently go over to the port side. She heeled immediately to port and half the men on deck, including Wilson and Sims, were thrown over into the water. Some of them, in falling or diving off, struck Kerr, who hurriedly backed away. Once off, most of them swam back to get on again, but Sims had had enough and he swam away, seeing as he did so the *Royal Oak* rolling over and the flash of a last explosion somewhere near the quarter-deck. Boxall, who was still hanging on by the funnel of the picket boat, estimated that less than six minutes had elapsed since the second explosion and thought, quite correctly, that she sank partly on her starboard side. Apart from the *Daisy*, and a few battered rafts and bits of wood, the picket boat was the only hope for the badly wounded men among the swimmers.

Kerr heard someone calling for help but, himself terribly burned, could do no more than urge the man on. 'Come on,' he shouted, 'only a few more yards.'

'I can't do it, I can't do it,' cried the man but, with Kerr shouting encouragement, by a supreme effort he eventually made the side of the picket boat.

Saltmarsh was out in the darkness, blinded by oil fuel and sick from having swallowed some of it; he had been sitting on the bottom of the ship when someone behind said, 'Get into the water, you silly bastard!' and gave him a push. 'I landed,' said Saltmarsh, 'in a whacking great pool of sludge, and got a bellyful of it.' Struggling blindly, he heard a voice calling, 'Make for the pinnace,' then felt himself dragged up by the arms. Still unable to see a thing, he found himself sitting on what felt like cushions, presumably in the stern sheets of the picket boat, and heard men shouting, 'We're overloaded, we've got too many as it is.'

Wilson had fallen overboard at the first lurch, at last losing the torch to which he had so tenaciously clung, but had climbed back on again, only to hear once more a shout of 'Trim the dish!' As men tried to move over to the starboard side, the port side came level, then rose higher – and the picket boat turned over.

Saltmarsh, still completely blind, found himself threshing about in the water, worried by his oil-filled jersey, which felt like an 'armour-plated jacket.' He struggled out of it, at once felt the intense cold – and felt something bump against him. It seemed to be a horsehair cushion from the picket boat. He grabbed at it and lost consciousness.

Wilson came to the surface amid a tremendous free-for-all of howling, screaming men. Arms grabbed hold of him and he found himself well down under the water, gripped by two men. He did not remember much of the struggle except that he managed to shove them off him and that when he broke surface all his clothes had gone – all he was wearing was a waistbelt and one leg of his pyjama trousers. He struck away at once from the circle of shouting, threshing, drowning swimmers.

On the edge of the arc it was quieter, there were only a few swimmers. He saw some of them throw up their hands and drown. One man said something like, 'Sorry, mate, sorry,' before he disappeared. Wilson knew he must not get too far away, or he would never be found. He began to feel the cold. 'It got past my flesh,' he said, 'until I could feel my own skeleton. I was aware of every bone in my body.'

Boxall jumped clear as the picket boat went over, but, seeing that she was still afloat, with an air-lock in her compartments, he swam back and got onto the keel. There must have been at that moment some thirty or forty men trapped inside, upside down. Many more swimmers came to join him, clambering up out of the water at the stem. So many climbed up that, within a minute or so, she sank stern first and disappeared for ever. Boxall went back into the water and swam around for a while, until he found a boat's chock to hold on to.

Somewhere about this time Mrs Evelyn Booth, 700 miles to the south, wakened from sleep by a disturbing dream, lay listening to the wind howling round the house in Southsea. What was the dream? She could not remember, but it had been about her husband and he was somehow safe from something. There had been a loud noise, too. But perhaps that had really been the blackout curtain, blown down by the wind. Somehow comforted, she turned over and went to sleep again.

George Booth, whose last memory had been of lying across a ladder inside the *Royal Oak.* and of tremendous waves of noise in his ears, recovered consciousness to find himself in the water, with what seemed to be half a gale blowing; it was very dark and cold, and he was stark naked, clutching a cigarette lighter in his hand. Dimly, he remembered that it was a present from his wife, arrived in the post the day before. He swam slowly, hardly conscious of what he was doing. After a little while, he saw another man in the water; curiously, the man was swimming with only one arm. As Booth went towards him, he recognised a friend – and saw, too, at the man's shoulder, a mess of flesh and bone where the left arm had been. Before Booth could do or say anything, the dying Sergeant cried out, 'Cheerio, chaps,' threw up his one arm, and sank.

McLaverty was trying to save a Maltese, who was shouting and crying out; he grabbed him by the shirt, saying, 'What's up, Joe?' But the Maltese was frantic, and kept turning over and over in the water, threshing wildly, until his shirt – which McLaverty still had hold of – was twisted like a rope. The Mediterranean was no sort of training for a swim in Scapa Flow in winter. McLaverty got his legs round the Maltese, trying to keep his head above the water that way, and calling out, 'Why don't you speak to me, Josie?' But the man gave no reply and in a little while was as stiff as a poker, with McLaverty's hand frozen to his shirt.

Finley, his burns caked now in oil, was too weak to swim far. Most of the time he just trod water and tried to keep up; above all, he wanted to keep the oil out of his mouth. At first there were terrible cries all around him, then they died away to an ominous silence. Two men appeared, splashing towards him. They asked if he could help them, but Finley managed to reply that he could hardly help himself. They made no attempt to grab hold of him, but carried on hopelessly, obviously not likely to last much longer.

Finley felt his strength ebbing, and was half resigned to going under, when he seemed to see green fields and felt, almost audibly, something saying, 'It's not your turn – keep going.' It was a sort of conscious hallucination, for he was seeing and hearing it in his mind – there was a face in it somewhere, too – and he was aware also, all the time, of his family and the need to keep alive for them. Just after that had put heart into him, a mast or spar came by, with a man sitting on the middle of it and another man on one end. This was real enough, and Finley caught hold of the free end, but he never did find out who the other two men were.

Almost immediately he saw a light – it was the *Daisy*, lying stopped – and they began to work their way towards it. When only a few yards away, the mast began to roll; the man at the far end vanished and did not reappear. Then Finley felt arms round him, lifting him, and solid deck under his feet; someone was saying, 'This chap's pretty bad.' He was put into the Skipper's bunk and Gatt himself, with all his other worries, turned the blankets so that the woollen side would not stick to his flesh. Finley knew only that he was in the Skipper's bunk but Gatt remembered him, because the burnt flesh was hanging in strips down his arms. Finley recalled asking for a drink of water, and of sitting up and looking at LSA Sims. Sims had a lifebelt on, and Finley shouted, 'Where'd you get that from?'

'I remember nothing else,' he said, 'except a Lieutenant having a terrible attack of hysterics, laughing and that; and people trying to calm him down. There was no pain yet – I just felt horrible. The oil was keeping my burns covered and I couldn't see what had happened to me.'

Booth, floating in the water, suddenly felt a sharp pain under his armpit, and found the *Daisy* above him and a man with a boat-hook hauling him to the side. Very far gone indeed, he was laid down on something cold and soft. When he revived enough to look round, he saw that it was a pile of oil-soaked corpses. He noticed an arm moving feebly, and dragged the man clear – the face looked as if soot had been forced into it, so terrible were the burns. That feeble movement was almost the last; the man died within a few minutes.

McLaverty also was too far gone to see the *Daisy*, he only heard the thud-thud of an engine and a shout, 'Get ahold of this line.' He never could have grasped it but, being wet, it wrapped itself round his right arm. 'They pulled me up like a shark, ripping me on the barnacles; I felt that, with salt water in the cuts.' At that moment, the body of the Maltese, long-since frozen stiff, fell away from McLaverty's grasp as the man's shirt tore.

The cold was so intense that even the strong swimmers were glad to get hold of any sort of support in the water; most of those who were afloat for any length of time, and survived, had found something to keep them up while they swam. Cadet Owen and a young Marine clung to the same piece of wood, and just waited to be found. Barry Hawes also had a bit of wood, but when he saw that another man a few yards away had a lifebelt, he asked if he could share it. Then, together, each with one arm locked in the lifebelt, they swam for the drifter. Sergeant Parham, not a good swimmer, thought he was in luck when a wave bounced something off his head and he found that it was a lifebelt. Even so, the real seriousness of his position, prior to that, never really struck home. When picked up, he threw back the lifebelt for someone else. Most of the men, now, had to be hauled out; if a line was thrown and they grabbed it, they usually fell back at the last moment. Paymaster Commander Cundall, burned but still wearing his cap, twice saw the *Daisy* turn away from him at the last moment to rescue someone else; Flag-Lieutenant Affleck-Graves pulled him aboard. Able Seaman Farley had been clinging to a bit of wood for two-and-a-half hours when he was found; too far gone to swim, he could still shout. 'Keep shouting,' yelled a voice out of the darkness, 'we'll find out where you are, then.' A line was thrown to him, but he was too weak even to grasp it, so a *Royal Oak* man, it may have been Batterbury, jumped again into the icy water with a line and tied it round Farley, who, so he said, was just about ready to hand in his Insurance Policy. As he was hauled up, he was recognised, and there was a delighted shout of 'Oh, it's you, you fat so-and-so!'

There was at least one boat floating water-logged; this was the gig, with its cover still in place. A number of survivors describe seeing it, and say they were the only person there, which is probable, because no one stayed long on it, it was warmer in the icy water. Some said it was floating right way up, and others upside down; and that, too, was quite possible, for it turned over on the slightest provocation. Engineer Commander Renshaw reached it early on, when the propellers of the capsized battleship were still faintly visible against the night sky. He estimated he was there forty-five minutes, sometimes on the canopy and sometimes on the keel. Stanley Rowlands passed it, and thought he saw a number of men trying to get on. Not a strong swimmer, and now with his foot broken, he had tried for five minutes to keep a young Marine afloat. The man made no move to help himself and Rowlands thought he was probably dead, and left him. After seeing the boat he remembered nothing more until, several hours later, he found himself in the *Daisy*.

After a long time, Renshaw saw the *Daisy* and remembered that he still had his torch in his pocket. He pulled it out and, to his surprise, it worked, so he flashed it on-and-off in the direction of the drifter. Eventually she steamed towards him and, when she was a hundred yards away, he slipped into the water and swam towards her. It may well have been Renshaw who gave Skipper Gatt the fright of his life.

'When we had about 250 survivors on board,' wrote Gatt a few months later, 'I thought the game was up; for, when I looked out on our port side, there was a light coming through the water, and I thought it was a torpedo. But it turned out to be a sailor with a lighted torch in his mouth, so you may know the relief that came to me when I saw what it was.' The light must have seemed curious, for the torch was covered in oil.

The gig was now abandoned, and Boxall was probably the next to reach it. He had first tried the picket boat, then a piece of wood; the gig proved equally unsatisfactory. 'I was sitting on the bows,' said Boxall, 'only my stern sheets in the water; but I got so cold there, in the wind, that I got back into the water again. Around me was only black darkness; I heard plenty of shouting, but couldn't see any lights.' He never saw the *Daisy* at all, until he was pulled on board and put in the wheel-house. Only one other man went into the wheelhouse, because Skipper Gatt needed room to con the drifter in the darkness.

Wilson was next to find the gig; he saw it first as a dark shadow in the water, riding submerged and waterlogged. He climbed on, got his chest out of the water, then, like Boxall, decided it was warmer in the icy sea, and simply hung on to its side. He did see the lights of the *Daisy* but, as she was approaching him, she went off on another tack. When she eventually came back, he heard a shout of, 'There he is.' Men leaned over him and started to hoist him in over the bows, but his numbed hands could no longer grip, and he fell back into the water, to a disgusted shout of, 'Don't muck around in the acquatic!' He had been in the water one-and-a-half hours.

The strain on Gatt was immense. With every boat gone and only one intact Carley raft afloat, the whole burden of saving life fell on him. As hour succeeded hour, peering out into the darkness to avoid ramming the wreck, manoeuvring a few yards towards faint voices coming from here, there and everywhere, and going below to see the wounded attended to, he became desperately tired. There was still no sign of life in the Flow, it was all entirely up to him. In all, he saved 386 men – almost all the survivors owed their lives to him and his crew.

At least fifty men tried to swim to the shore, half-a-mile away, but less than twenty reached it. Although it was a calm night, there was a bad 'lop' on the water; the north-east wind, coming from over the cliffs, blew the tops of the waves into the swimmers' faces when they tried to go in that direction. Petty Officer Kerr, after leaving the picket boat, found himself alone, 'it seemed on a wide, wide sea,' but got a mouthful of water when he struck out for the shore. So he turned round and breast-stroked in the opposite direction which was much easier. If he had headed a little further to the left he would have gone out into the middle of Scapa Flow and drowned somewhere in the gloom. Eventually he saw two white lights, which did not move; as he went slowly towards them two men paddled past him on a piece of wreckage – probably part of a Carley float – and disappeared into the darkness. At length, labouring badly, he saw that the lights were actually the anchor lights of a fairly large ship. It was the *Pegasus*. With the skin burnt off his head, neck and hands, he had swum two miles in icy water, and had taken at least two hours and forty-five minutes to do it.

By 3.55, two-and-a-half hours after the sinking, there was silence around the *Daisy*; there were no more voices calling from the water. The drifter was dangerously full of men and many of them needed medical attention urgently. Skipper Gatt decided to discontinue the search and take the survivors to the *Pegasus*. At about this time, or shortly after he left the scene, two whalers from the *Pegasus* arrived in the area and began to search with torches. Some of the survivors were later told that the peculiar actions of the *Daisy* had at last aroused attention and that the boats had been sent to investigate. Skipper Gatt states categorically that, until he brought the *Daisy* alongside the gangway of the *Pegasus*, 'they didn't know a rap about what was going on.' And he estimates that it took him at least fifteen minutes to reach her. The time, then, was 4.10 a.m., or a few minutes after.

The *Pegasus* immediately switched on a signal projector, which briefly swept the water towards where the *Royal Oak* had been; it blazed in short flashes only, as it was not designed for continuous burning. The men in the intact Carley raft saw it, but it did not illuminate them. Bendell, still swimming, saw it, too; it went backwards and forwards across the water, but did not reach him. It did, however, enable him to see, for the first time, that there was another man near him in the water; his head was black with oil-fuel and, as Bendell made towards him, he went under suddenly and did not reappear.

Kerr, labouring towards the anchor lights of the *Pegasus*, saw that there was a drifter alongside the gangway, the *Daisy* disembarking survivors. Batterbury, from the landing stage, was helping to pull an injured Paymaster out of the water, he thought it might have been Lieutenant-Commander Maclean. At the same time, other men were helping a terribly burned man onto the landing stage; from the description it was Instance. 'It sticks in my mind,' said Batterbury, 'flesh was running like water from his hands and face, more from the hands than the face. He was holding them in front of him, like downward-pointing claws, and the flesh was dripping off them. I remember being genuinely surprised at what burning could do: I had no idea anything like this happened. I also remember feeling astonished because he was not in pain – at any rate, not to the extent of the damage done to him. He didn't howl, but just acted as you would if you'd jammed your finger in something. I seem to remember they covered him with a blanket.'

Instance, who had arrived on the buckled Carley raft, perhaps the one Kerr had seen go past him, was not in fact conscious at that moment; or, at any rate, has no memory of it. But he did recall what happened less than a minute later, as he was being taken to the gangway. He heard a seaman say, 'He's got a belt round his waist.' Another seaman answered, 'Sling it away, then we'll get a blanket over him.'

Instance sat up with a jerk. 'Not on your nelly,' he shouted, 'my money's in that!'

But Kerr screamed out in pain when two men knelt down from the landing stage and grabbed him by the hands. He heard one of them call, 'Throw down a line, he's a big chap.' They put the line round him and hoisted his fifteen-and-a-half stone weight on to the *Daisy*. 'Then it started,' said Kerr, 'I began to tremble and shiver with cold and shock.'

Instance and Kerr, like all the men who had been burnt, were not in pain until someone touched them; they merely felt weak and ill, and shivered uncontrollably. The agony was reserved for later.

CHAPTER TEN

'REGRET *ROYAL OAK* HAS SUNK'

In accordance with instructions for patrol duties, Police Constable David H Allan called in at Kirkwall Police Station during the early hours of the morning, while these scenes were taking place a few miles away; but he cannot now remember exactly the time. While there, a telephone call came through which resulted in his being told to go out with another constable, wake a local bus hirer, and get a bus sent to Scapa Pier as quickly as possible. As they were hurrying along they met a civilian, who told them that the *Royal Oak* had been sunk.

While he was doing this, Edwin Wheeler, sleeping in the water-boat *Fountain* which was tied up to Lyness stone jetty, was woken by a Lieutenant-Commander or Commander who was asking for the Master of the vessel. Very shortly afterwards the *Fountain* raised steam and began to move up through the destroyer anchorage towards Rysa Sound and Hoy Sound, which held at this moment a number of coasters being used as store ships. They stopped at each one and passed the order, 'Raise steam and prepare to leave Scapa at one hour's notice.' They were now told by the Master that the *Royal Oak* had sunk at her anchorage.

The reason for all this minor activity was that three survivors, having swum half a mile to the shore, had still sufficient strength left to walk the two miles to Scapa and wake the Pier Master. He telephoned the *Iron*

Duke, ten miles away at Lyness, and she made to *Pegasus*, 'What has happened?' *Pegasus* promptly sent back, 'Regret *Royal Oak* has sunk.'

The fishing drifters at Scapa Pier were getting up steam; some of them concentrated their search close inshore along the rocky cliffs opposite the sunken battleship and were later joined by one of the whalers from the *Pegasus*. They cruised slowly along, calling out in the night to anyone who might be lying on the rocks. Here and there came back an answer.

When Stoker Cleverley, still unaware of his burns, went off from the starboard side of the quarter-deck, he found himself among a group of perhaps fifty men. Among them was a Lieutenant who called out to them, 'No use waiting for boats – swim to the shore.' And off, they went. Among them were Boy E W Scovell and Ordinary Seaman R ('Pincher') Martin, both of whom are now Lieutenants. Scovell was one of the strong swimmers; perfectly at home in the water, he spent most of his holidays swimming and had competed for his school. Apart from the cold and the oil, it was an easy twenty-minute swim, the 'lop' which bothered the moderate swimmers and the badly injured was of no real account to anyone used to swimming head down, mouth under water most of the time. He plugged on steadily until he saw ahead of him the fluorescence where the waves were breaking on the rocks. After he had climbed out of the water, it was very cold; he just huddled there on his own, trying to keep warm.

Cleverley had a rough idea of the direction to take, and after a while could make out the dim loom of the cliffs; behind him in the Flow it was quite dark, with no land to be seen. He remembers nothing more until he was climbing up the rocks; after getting perhaps ten feet out of the water he collapsed and lost consciousness, he had no idea why.

Lieutenant Keen had never before swum more than a hundred yards. But soon after skidding down the quarter-deck and being pitched into the sea, he found a bit of wood and locked his arms round it while he kicked out with his feet. His first instinct, thinking of the *Vanguard*, was to get away; next, he was obsessed with a fear that he might swim right out of the Flow, through Hoxa Sound, so he turned left for the shore. He took a long time to reach it and, if he had not found the wood, certainly would never have done so. 'I was getting rather numb,' is how he described it, 'as though I was slowly going to sleep, there was no discomfort or anything. I was mentally and physically tired, not really thinking of anything, not cold, not frightened, not uncomfortable, just doing a sort of breast stroke with the wood under my arms.'

Even so, there were reserves of strength. 'I suddenly woke up in a very vigorous way, because I heard waves breaking. It was pretty calm, so I knew I must be near to shore, and I suddenly swam like mad. I must have clashed into the rocks, because I remember my head banging against them. I came to, with a few cuts on face and head, jolly pleased at having something solid to hold on to.'

For a while Keen lay there, half in and half out of the water, then he started to climb – the rocks were sharp and hard to his bare feet – tripped, and fell over a Boy seaman. Both of them were totally exhausted and covered in oil. After a rest, they began to climb the cliff, hoping to make their way inland and find a farm; but they were as weak as kittens and, in the dark, the attempt appeared dangerous. Someone else, to their left, was also scrambling up, to judge by the noises; the sounds ended abruptly in a cry and a thump.

That decided them to wait for daylight, so they huddled together for warmth. Then they saw, only a few feet away, two white circles moving closer towards them. It was a second or so before Keen realised that it was the whites of a man's eyes. They asked the apparition who it was, and it said that it was Leading Telegraphist so-and-so. He was completely black with oil and even at a distance of two feet only his eyes could be seen. They all lay down, to get as much out of the wind as possible, and drifted off into unconsciousness.

Out in the Flow, four hours after the sinking, SBA Bendell was still afloat. A strong swimmer, now a member of Portsmouth Lifeguards, he too had made for the shore; but came suddenly into a patch of oil fuel which not only stank but clogged his movements. 'It was as if someone was holding on to me, trying to drag me back, a ghastly feeling; I was more frightened then than at any time.' He had in fact been injured while scrambling out of the submerged compartment. He gave up the attempt and merely tried to keep in the patches of clear water, shouting for help. He saw the signal projector come on in the *Pegasus* – by then it must have been about 4.15 a.m. and he was hoarse with shouting, so he stopped. Eventually he saw a boat, a whaler from the *Pegasus*, and grabbed at an oar which they held out to him. He was told afterwards that he had been picked up at about 6 a.m. During his time in the water he had had nothing whatever to hold on to and had exceeded by two hours his allotted 'expectation of life,' possibly because of the oil.

The survivors on the Commander's raft and the Captain's half-raft had already been picked up by the whalers. Blundell did not wait for that, he was already fed up with the people who wanted to head for the *Pegasus*, when he knew very well the shore was only quarter-of-a-mile away; he swam over to the whaler, leaving them to go round in circles without him. When the whaler did arrive, it was unable to take all the men on and around the raft, and quite a number were left behind, including the injured Fossey. After a long delay, another boat picked them up. Fossey remembers being covered by a blanket and another survivor trying to pull it off him; also someone saying to the man, 'You touch him again, and we'll throw you over the side.'

Some time between 4 and 5 o'clock Cleverley was woken up by shouting. A whaler was coming along by the rocks, with men calling out, 'Anyone there?' He shouted back, and was taken off. A few minutes later they found Scovell who, because they could not risk the boat by coming close inshore at that point, had to swim out to them. They were all feeling rather light-headed now that they were safe. When Scovell gave his name 'Pincher' Martin, who had also reached the land and was already in the boat, bellowed out, 'You can throw that back!'

Somewhere nearby they could hear splashing – it was probably another man who had got ashore previously, Scovell had heard him shouting. Now, they thought, he must be trying to swim out to the whaler. They looked, but never found him. There were reports afterwards of a number of sailors found dead on the shore, their arms outstretched as if to grasp the rocks. Constable Allan was in fact called down a few days afterwards to one such body, naked and covered in oil fuel. 'My thoughts were,' he said, 'that this poor fellow probably saved himself from the sea that tragic morning, but had dropped exhausted on reaching the shore, and died of exposure.'

The most curious thing about it all, thought Cleverley later, was that, after first being burned, then thrown into the icy sea, and finally exposed naked for hours to a bitter wind, he himself suffered not even so much as a cold, let alone pneumonia; nor did anyone else that he heard of.

Eventually the whaler had some seven or eight men on board, and transferred them to a fishing drifter which had come out from Scapa to help. When trying to get warm on the engine room gratings, Cleverley discovered for the first time that he had been burnt – he was a hospital case for more than three weeks afterwards – and that he was still holding in his hand the sodden box of matches which he had grabbed from above his hammock just before the third explosion.

At Scapa Pier a crowd was waiting. Constable Allan was now there with the civilian bus and Cleverley was carried to it; he was rather resentful, he felt quite all right. They were wrapped in white blankets, and he thought what a shame it was to ruin them. Fifteen men in all were landed at Scapa Pier and taken to the Kirkwall Hotel, which had been requisitioned by the Navy. Cleverley found himself perched on a chair by the fire, with his legs up, opposite Chief Stoker C Hine. Anything they liked to drink, they could have. 'Lofty and I sat there drinking whisky as if it was water, and talking. I had no eyebrows, my hair was all gone on one side, my right ear was burnt, also my feet and lower legs.' People crowded round, bombarding them with questions; their names were taken and, within a few hours, these fifteen became the first list of, survivors to be issued by the Admiralty.

Constable Allan helped to get some of them out to the Naval aerodrome at Hatston, where Cleverley was put in what he thought was the Sub-Lieutenants' dormitory. 'I didn't have much time for officers,' he said, 'but those Fleet Air Arm people were very good; they got us a radio, and one of them gave me his pyjama jacket, which was all I had in the way of clothes.'

Meanwhile, Keen and the two others with him had missed their chance of figuring in the first list. He woke up, becoming conscious of a light, and crawled to the edge of the rocks. A fishing drifter was close inshore, shining an Aldis lamp up and down the cliffs; closer inshore still was the drifter's dingy. Keen crawled back to wake the other two. 'I was beastly to them,' he said, 'I kept hitting and thumping them, but they didn't stir.' He turned to call out to the two men in the dingy and a braw Scots voice replied, 'Aw reet, we're here.'

Then he was in the stokehold of the drifter. 'The three of us were sitting there like three old black crows by the furnace; I, very well-dressed in my pyjamas, the Boy in a vest and one sock, the Leading Tel. in one sock. A man who was down there, doing the coaling and answering the telegraph,' handed us a huge mug of tea – with something in it. I told him about the chap I'd heard falling down the cliff, and he shouted the information up the voice-pipe to the Skipper.' A search revealed nothing and the drifter took them, not to Scapa Pier, but out to the *Pegasus*.

The Fleet water-carrier *Fountain* took some three hours to complete her task of alerting the store ships and colliers by word-of-mouth. For the first part of the trip the *Royal Oak*'s anchorage, ten miles to the northeast, was hidden from her view by the island of Fara, but, as she steamed into Gutter Sound, Edwin Wheeler could look right across. They had all expected to see some form of activity, but there was nothing, neither searchlights nor the lights of ships were visible; it was all absolutely dark and quiet.

In fact there were a few drifters and boats cruising over the spot, with dimmed riding lights, searching for survivors with the aid of nothing larger than a torch. The *Pegasus*, after briefly switching on a signal lamp, had thought better of it and blacked out again. At about this time Midshipman Pirie was listening to what he called a 'slight altercation' between a senior officer from the *Royal Oak* and a senior officer of the *Pegasus*. The *Royal Oak* officer was demanding to know why the *Pegasus* had not switched on a searchlight, and the other was replying, equally forcibly, that he did not wish to be torpedoed as well.

On the other hand, the two destroyers at Lyness remained where they were and no search for a submarine was made until daylight, and this may have been partly because there were other, more plausible, reasons for the disaster being canvassed at that moment. Engineer Commander Renshaw, after a hot bath, went into the wardroom in borrowed clothing and met there Captain Bonn and Commander Nichols. Although his first assumption had been that it was a torpedo, the discussion unearthed other possibilities. The *Royal Oak* was the fifth British warship to blow up at anchor – they all remembered the other four cases during the first world war, one of them actually in Scapa. Those never had been explained, although certain alterations to magazines had afterwards been put in hand. In particular, they remembered HMS *Natal*, which had blown up at Invergordon a few hours after a children's party had been held on board, during which, quite naturally, a number of nonservice personnel had been in the ship. They were all very much aware of the similarity between that and the storing of the *Royal Oak* a few hours previously. Wherever stores had been put, there had been an explosion; and there was, too, that disquieting gap of twelve minutes between the first explosion and the second, which did not fit at all with the short gaps of a torpedo salvo but did fit the irregular, unpredictable workings of acid in the fuses of time bombs.

Another conjecture was that an aircraft had laid a string of mines in the anchorage and that the ship had swung at her anchor over them; the tide had in fact been on the turn at about that time. No certain conclusion could be reached, but the general impression was that the *Royal Oak* had been sunk by, as the Flag-Lieutenant expressed it, 'an unknown agency.' There was a good deal of gloom; if Hitler could do this to them, what would happen to the rest of the Fleet?

The *Pegasus* was the ex-*Ark Royal*, 6,900 tons, purchased as a seaplane tender in 1914, and now used for transporting aircraft. She was quite the most distinctive ship in the Navy – once seen, never forgotten – with her single spindly funnel and mast apparently in the wrong place. She was not equipped, as a depot ship would have been, to deal with a sudden influx of 400 sodden, oil-soaked, shocked and wounded men; but she coped magnificently. Her crew gave up their hammocks, their clothes and their kit to the survivors; they turned on hot baths, made tea and cocoa, and poured out rum. They sorted out the unhurt from the wounded, and the badly wounded from the men able to walk, they took names and addresses for notifying next-of-kin, they asked the hospital ship *Saint Abba* to send her drifter to take off the urgent cases, and they notified Kirkwall that additional medical supplies would be needed.

By 6 a.m. all the survivors were out of the *Daisy* and being dealt with in the *Pegasus*. Captain Benn then asked Skipper Gatt to go back to the scene of the sinking for a further search, but as fishing drifters from Scapa were now moving about over the spot Gatt thought it was unnecessary; he also thought he had done enough for one night (the Admiralty agreed, they gave him the DSC). Shortly after, an ex-fishing drifter, fitted out as a tender to the hospital ship, arrived alongside and began to embark the badly injured. She was so new that the bunks had no mattresses or pillows.

Surgeon Commander G L Ritchie now began to get the worst cases into her. Himself a survivor, he had taken a leading part in looking after the wounded. 'How that man worked!' said Kerr, who, wrapped in blankets and hot-water bottles and filled with brandy, was still trembling uncontrollably. He was helped down the gangway, gave his name, rating and number to a Marine corporal standing there, and was put into a small cabin with five other men, including Supply Petty Officer Finley, Able Seaman Handforth and Ordinary Seaman Hearn. Then Sick Berth Attendant Bendell was brought in. He had been in the water much longer than most and was suffering from the shock of being trapped inside the ship when she went down; he had hurt his feet and hands badly and was afraid of losing a finger. He was muttering all the time, 'Don't take it off, don't take it off!' Dommett, unable to walk, was slung into what had been the fish-hold, now equipped with bunks, and squirmed around trying to make a pillow for himself. Instance was just beginning to revive and to feel the pain of his burns – an agony which was to last for many weeks. The men in the cabin were trying rather comically to help each other with drinks and cigarettes, fumbling because their hands were raw. At about 8.15 the drifter got under way for Lyness, where the hospital ship was lying.

Meanwhile, those who could walk had been sent down to the engine and boiler rooms to warm up. Chief Stoker Lawrence, injured, was half carried in by two seamen but, as soon as he saw a boiler, he flung them off and curled himself round it. He was badgered to drink cocoa, but refused; accepted a cup of coffee and was immediately sick. After that he felt better. McLaverty was given rum – and then struck violently in the stomach. He, too, was sick; and felt better. Batterbury was handed a glass, drank it – and found it was salt water. That, too, had the desired effect. Farley was given hot water – and vomited. What came up was, he said, 'just like ink.' It was, of course, oil fuel. 'They knew what they were doing, all right,' said Batterbury, wryly. Lieutenant Keen finished the best part of a bottle of whisky within an hour – it had absolutely no effect, presumably because of his oil-lined stomach; then, trailing 'blood and cinders' from the cuts on his feet, went to look for survivors from the Royal Marine detachment. There were pitifully few.

Saltmarsh found himself looking up at some sort of light, rather like the sun seen through closed eyelids; as his last recollection was of holding onto a cushion in the night near the capsized picket boat, he was puzzled. He was still in the water, but now it was hot. He was in fact being bathed. Some time later, it may have been days later, he was in a cabin with a man bending over him saying, 'Who are you, son?' All he could reply was, 'I'm a Marine, I'm a Marine.'

The idea of the hot baths was to restore lost heat to the body as well as to remove the oil fuel, but some time during the night the hot water gave out. Blundell, who had to be carried to the bathroom, was simply wiped down. His clothes were thrown on to a rapidly growing pile of filthy, oil-stained garments. Then he was put straight into somebody else's hammock and went off to sleep.

One man, Farley says he was a Scotsman, actually wasted hot water; naked, he was standing under a tap washing a bundle of pound notes. When Lawrence came to, the first man he saw was the Schoolmaster – 'a tall, portly person, he was striding gravely about the boiler-room, as naked as the day he was born, except for his shoes.' Within half-an-hour Blundell woke up again, vaguely uneasy; then he remembered that his money belt – with the £13 1s. in it – had been thrown onto the heap of filthy clothing. The heap was much larger when he got back to it, but he tore into the pile and found the belt. Much satisfied, he marched back to his hammock.

CHAPTER ELEVEN

'Believed by U-Boat Action'

After breakfast – and a 'Red' air raid warning, which was probably a reconnaissance aircraft – the *Pegasus* got under way for Lyness, where she transferred the survivors to the SS *Voltaire*, a former Lamport and Holt liner. They were now among the islands, with the naval base in full view; nearby were the *Saint Abba*, the *Iron Duke*, two destroyers, a collier, and a number of store ships and auxiliaries. As Farley shuffled over the brow into the *Voltaire*, holding up with one hand a pair of trousers much too small for him, he said 'Good morning' to a padre standing there to welcome them, and was told that he was the happiest survivor the padre had seen that day – a sight for sore eyes. Then he was given 'a good hot breakfast, with lashings of rum,' and went off in search of a bathroom. The oil, he said, was oozing out of him for two weeks afterwards.

Intent on a second breakfast, Lieutenant Keen came into the mess, which was of course new to him, and saw a number of strange faces, the *Voltaire*'s officers. A grumpy old Commander asked him who he was, so Keen replied that he was ex-*Royal Oak*. 'Sabotage!' grunted the Commander. 'I thought so! Always said it would happen.' No one said a word, that was what they all feared it was.

During the rest of the morning and afternoon there was steady methodical activity in the Flow; minesweepers were at work, searching for a possible submarine or for any torpedoes which had missed their target, and picket boats armed with a single depth-charge balanced on the stern were cruising about. Nothing was found, except the Barrel of Butter buoy, several times reported as a conning-tower. And that was odd.

Assuming that a submarine *had* got in, then the first explosion – twelve minutes before the others – must have represented a bare hit right up in the bows from a salvo of three or four. Where were the missing two or three torpedoes? And if they had struck the rocks and exploded, why had no one heard? Those would have been really visible, audible explosions – unlike the muffled internal-sounding thumps which had sunk the *Royal Oak*. More curious still, assuming the explosion in the inflammable store to be a torpedo hit on the bow, then it had hit by a margin of a few feet only and the other torpedoes in the salvo had missed completely. As the *Royal Oak* was lying with her starboard side to the land, then the submarine must have fired from less than half-a-mile away at a huge, stationary target – and missed it. Even those who had heard 'Pony' Moore say that he could bring in a submarine through Kirk Sound thought that this particular affair had nothing to do with submarines.

The men were equally depressed; most of them were convinced that the explosions had been internal, and they thought they knew what had caused them. Marine Owens believed that, while swimming with a Midshipman, he had seen the conning-tower, and part of the hull of a submarine a hundred yards away. However, it was a dark night, it might easily have been an optical illusion, possibly the gig floating upside down with a man astride the keel. 'Sabotage' was the virtually unanimous conclusion. Paradoxically and illogically, proof that they had been torpedoed would improve morale one hundred per cent. Sabotage, it was felt, could occur anywhere, any time, whereas if a submarine had got through some gap, then the gap could be closed. In the circumstances, a submarine it had to be, whether it was or not.

During the morning – it was still Saturday the 14th – the Admiralty announced that the *Royal Oak* had been lost, 'believed by U-boat action,' and issued the first fifteen names of survivors. At the same time, they ordered an immediate concentration of divers at Scapa Flow. The battleship lay bottom up but heeled over partly onto her starboard side in about 100 feet of water, so that at low tide her port bilges showed above the surface. A Fleet Air Arm pilot, who had just flown over her, came into the dormitory at Hatston aerodrome where Cleverley was, and told them that the *Royal Oak* had 'four big holes in her that you could drive a bus through.'

An examination of those holes would soon prove whether the explosions had been internal or external; further, if she had been sunk by torpedoes, undeniable proof, in the shape of bits of them, would be lying around waiting to be picked up. The parts, if they were there, would also be of interest to the Admiralty's Torpedo Experimental Establishment at Greenock. But, if the mine-sweepers could find a complete, unexploded torpedo, that would be even better. The missing torpedoes were never found, either then or later.

The news of the sinking was reported in *BBC* news bulletins late in the morning, and repeated. The statement that fifteen survivors had been landed was taken by many anxious relatives to mean that there had been *only* fifteen. Afternoon newspapers carried the story on their front pages, under flaring headlines – apart from the *Courageous*, it was the first big-ship loss – and gave the names of the fifteen. This was all the news they had; they filled in with statistics, history of the ship, and the last-known list of senior officers. The Germans picked up the continual *BBC* announcements and began to repeat them, adding that nothing about the operation was yet known in Germany. In the dockyard towns, particularly Portsmouth, where most of the men came from, crowds of friends and relatives gathered outside the RN Barracks to read the names as, hourly, fresh lists of survivors were put up. Most of them would not read there the name they hoped to see.

Mrs Parham, wife of the Sergeant gunnery instructor, did not turn on the radio that day. The *BBC*, geared to total war from the start, had liberally studded their programme plans with spaces for news announcements; those spaces had to be filled, whether or not there was any new news. People soon got tired of listening. During the afternoon Mrs Parham did not go out, so missed seeing the newspaper placards shouting '*Royal Oak* Sunk.' When a neighbour, who worked in the C-in-C's office, called to say, 'Your husband's safe,' Mrs Parham had no idea what she was talking about.

On the other hand, even before the first announcement, Mrs Booth, worried by her dream, tried to tell her mother about it. All she got was a refusal even to listen, on the grounds that a 'Friday night dream on a Saturday told' is bad luck. 'Well, he's safe, anyway!' she shouted at her mother's retreating back. At midday her sister came in with the news that the *Royal Oak* had gone, so she went with her baby son to Eastney Barracks to look at the lists of names. Her husband's name was not there. Anything might have happened, even a battle, for the Admiralty announcement made no mention of where or in what circumstances the battleship had been lost.

Mrs Walker, with two sons in the Navy, had also had a dream that night. She had woken her husband to say that she had dreamed of newsboys in the streets shouting, 'Loss of the *Royal Oak.*' Their youngest son, Cecil Edward Walker, aged sixteen, was serving in her. For Mrs Walker there was to be no name on a survivors' list.

Another mother of a sixteen-year-old son, Bugler Harry Mountford, RM, had at his request pleaded with the Drum Major to let him go to sea. She thought at the time that it meant only a two-year commission in the Mediterranean. He, too, was dead.

In the *Voltaire*, all that day, there were roll calls; name after name read out, and no answer.

Almost all the Boys had gone, except for a proportion of those in the battery. The Admiral was dead and the Gunnery Officer, Lieutenant-Commander Roper, with his second-in-command, 'Pony' Moore; so was Captain Edgar Balls, commanding the RM detachment. From Portsmouth alone, there were more than forty Marines lost. The Stokers had suffered particularly badly and the Maltese mess had been almost wiped out. Three of the men landed by the *Daisy* were dead on arrival or died shortly after; one of the wounded, Stoker Tate, was soon to die. Only a third of the ship's company remained. Twenty-four officers and 809 men had lost their lives.

In the *Voltaire*, a container of rum was broached; anyone who wanted to help himself could do so. For some survivors that was the highlight of the whole affair; but a surprisingly large number did not drink. That night, in the hospital ship, few of the badly burned men slept much, even when doped; it was the first sleepless night in an endless succession of tormented nights and days.

'Several of us wore a bandage mask on our faces,' wrote Petty Officer Kerr, while the memory was still vivid. 'There were two holes to see through and a slit for the mouth. Our mouths were swelled and blistered, the same as our faces, and all we kept on wanting was fluid to wet the mouth. We couldn't sleep with our pain and thoughts, and used to long for the morning to come. The night sister gave us shots of morphia that killed the pain for a while and we could sleep; but not for long, as I used to have the most terrifying dreams of that tragic morning. The doctor asked me one night how I felt, I expect he saw tears in my eyes, they were there, I know; I told him I could not help thinking about my old shipmates. He patted me on the shoulder and said, 'Try to get some sleep.'

On Sunday, the 5th, diving operations began. What the divers found there echoes still. There were bodies leaning out of the wreck, half in and half out of the port-holes; there were corpses in the hull, jammed by falling gear; and on the seabed, the bloated shapes of drowned swimmers floated more or less upright, executing in the tides a macabre undersea dance.

The bottom was of sand and such clouds arose, whenever a diver moved foot or hand, that they had to enter the riven darkness of the hull and work there in that mass tomb by touch alone. One of the divers, a Portsmouth man, had had a son in the *Royal Oak*; he was still in the hull. The father was not required to dive, but helped supervise from the surface. The scenes found below were still being passed on among the Orkney Defence Force years afterwards; it was said that divers had come up, crazed with horror.

But, apart from this, the divers did not talk. There was a security blanket on the work, which still lingers. Metal Industries (Salvage) Ltd., whose divers took part, as late as November, 1958, politely referred a request for information to the Admiralty. The diving boat, the survivors heard, was manned entirely by officers. HMS *Vernon*, the Navy's mine and diving establishment, supplied a large contingent. One of these men told a survivor, later, that he was flown up for the work, that he carried out one dive, made his report, was immediately flown back to Portsmouth, and two days afterwards flown out to Libya. Even if he did talk, no one diver could possibly recreate anything like a complete picture of the wreck or of the damage to it; for that, he would need to talk to other divers. Only on the basis of reports from many divers, working simultaneously on and around the hull, could a plan and, eventually, a model of the wreck be made.

Some information did leak, in due course, but to survivors only; unfortunately it was contradictory. Diver H told one survivor that he had found pieces of torpedo down there; Diver W told one survivor, and the wife of another, that he had found no traces of torpedo, that the plates were blown outwards, as from internal explosion, and that 'you could drive a double-decker bus through the hole.' Even nineteen years afterwards, these men would not be interviewed.

While this work, wrapped in strictest secrecy, went on, a simultaneous survey was being made of the fixed defences of Scapa Flow. There was no evidence to show that a submarine had got through the booms at Hoxa Sound, Switha Sound, or Hoy Sound. Surveys were then made of the eastern entrances closed by blockships; particular attention was paid to Kirk Sound, about which the dead Lieutenant Moore had made an official report. The channel was in fact navigable by surface vessels and in use by them; but a submarine, extremely hard to handle in a high-speed current bubbling round corners, which was the position here except at slack water, would be likely to strike a blockship and leave traces.

Chief Petty Officer E G Pratt, a naval pensioner called up a few months before, took part in the survey of Kirk Sound. Curiously enough, he, like McLaverty, had been in Scapa Flow when the *Vanguard* blew up, and remembered it vividly. While other people took soundings at high and low water, he got on with his job – which was to examine the blockships for any sign that a submarine had got through and grazed them in its passing, as it was very likely to do. He returned a nil report – 'Not a barnacle scratched off 'em.'

While the surveys were still going on a blockship arrived at Scapa – it was intended for Kirk Sound. It was a replacement for a blockship sent earlier, which had been sunk during its passage to Orkney. Even if it had got there, it would still have arrived after the outbreak of war; this was due partly to protracted negotiations with the Treasury, but only partly. The best outlay for the strictly limited amount of money available to them, was the responsibility of the Admiralty.

About two dozen bodies had been recovered from the Flow, indicating that the number drowned had been smaller than had at first appeared likely and that most of the 833 men lost had died inside the ship, while still trying to get out. Some of the two dozen even might have floated out of the wreck; and it was subsequently reported that nets had been placed over it to prevent this happening.

The dead men were brought to Lyness and a number of survivors were asked to identify them. Some, with a horror of recognising friends, refused to do it; Batterbury was one. But Sergeant Booth took part – the first man he saw was a senior Engineer; Farley took part – an Ordnance Artificer friend was lying there. All, said Farley, had died by drowning, there were no external wounds. On Monday, the 16th, they were buried in the naval cemetery at Lyness, among the crosses of the men who had died in the *Vanguard* and of Germans from the surrendered High Seas Fleet.

It was a cold, sunny day. As the long lines of survivors followed a bugler and a squad of ratings with rifles at the trail up the hill above Lyness, the sun was momentarily obscured by a passing cloud. Two men in the leading file of survivors carried wreaths; Behind them marched a motley array, few of whom were properly dressed. Mostly, they wore boiler suits and white gym shoes, issued in the *Voltaire*; many had white caps instead of black; some were wearing clothes given to them by the crews of the *Daisy* and the *Pegasus*. As the funeral party stood with reversed arms above the grave and the bugle notes rang over the hill, the sun, directly behind the ranks, shone out and cast their shadows across the raw earth.

During the day, news came in of an air raid on that part of the Home Fleet which was lying in the Firth of Forth, one of its alternative bases; the cruiser *Southampton* was hit by a bomb which did not explode and the destroyer *Mohawk* was damaged by splinters. Most of the heavy units were at another alternative base, Loch Ewe.

In the *Voltaire*, arrangements were being made to hold a Court of Enquiry next day; Vice-Admiral R H T Raikes had come to Scapa to conduct it. Statements had been taken from key witnesses. Cleverley, still at the aerodrome, had not been able to say much, except that he thought it was sabotage – which was not well received; Fossey had been interviewed by half-a-dozen officers who seemed to know a lot about it already. Captain Benn did not show himself much to the ratings in the *Voltaire*; for him the tragedy had been a crushing blow. At one moment he had been in command of a 39,000 ton battleship, the next he was unemployed, and likely to remain so if the verdict of the Court went against him. But he made a point of visiting the wounded in the *Saint Abba*. Fossey was the last man he came to in that particular ward; he asked if Fossey, who had been on watch, had seen the submarine. 'That shook me,' said Fossey, 'it was the first thing I'd heard about a submarine; and I don't think to this day it was.' After Captain Benn had gone, a buzz of excited talk broke out in the ward; this theory was new to them, too.

The gospel of a submarine was intensively spread by the officers, whatever their private thoughts; they publicly ridiculed all suggestions of sabotage. At this time, the minesweepers had recovered nothing – and never would do so – while the divers were investigating with such secrecy that, if the answer should be unwelcome, in the sense of being damaging to morale, it would never be known.

That evening an impromptu concert was organised in the *Voltaire*, to cheer people up; and the audience insisted on singing 'Daisy, Daisy' as a mark of gratitude to Skipper Gatt and his crew. In the *Saint Abba*, another tormented night began for the badly burned men.

Next day, Tuesday the 17th, Sergeant Booth went over to the *Iron Duke* for mail; he had asked to do this duty because his brother-in-law, a Chief Supply rating, was in her. The mail office was on her quarter-deck, in place of 'Y' turret, which had been removed when she was demilitarised. There was a bag of mail for the *Royal Oak* and Booth collected this. While he was away, Blundell was in the well-deck of the *Voltaire* with a party rigging it up for the Court of Enquiry; Lieutenant Benton was outside his cabin. Blundell heard the usual air raid warning 'Red.' Then he heard aero engines; he had never heard them before, the German reconnaissance aircraft always flew too high. But these sounded loud enough and the planes seemed to be diving. Then he saw them – three Heinkel 111s coming down in a long shallow dive at the ships in the Flow. Benton heard the whining roar of diving planes, then the stutter of machine-guns. 'Christ, this is it!' he thought, and ran on deck. Planes were going down on the *Iron Duke*, moored in Longhope, and more were coming in over the Flow, and starting to dive.

Blundell saw two bombs fall from the second Heinkel towards the *Iron Duke*; they looked about the size of kit-bags and they were jerking as they fell. An enormous wall of water rose up close alongside the battleship's stern and then subsided onto her quarter-deck – what might have been either bodies or mailbags went with it, when it poured back into the sea.

The *Saint Abba*, much nearer to the *Iron Duke* than the *Voltaire*, seemed to be directly under the attacking planes. 'It was horrible,' said Finley, 'because if the ship was hit, we were done, we couldn't do a thing about it.' A nurse stood beside Finley all the time, holding his hand, to calm him; she never flinched. Bendell, highly excited, scrambled out of his cot to a port, and began to shout a commentary. 'Look – here's another one coming down!' The rising metallic howl of aero engines passed over the hospital ship. 'Oh, they hit her that time!' More and more aircraft chundered over, beginning their dives from directly above the patients in the ward. All the AA guns were firing, and the high-pitched detonations mixed with the gutteral throb of engines and the whine of the diving aircraft. High above the racket rose the shrill, rising whistle of descending bombs, increasing to a howling shriek, and dissolving in the roar of explosions. The water heaved all round the *Saint Abba*, and the hospital ship rocked violently, the wounded swaying in their cots.

A sister dashed in, dragged Bendell away from the port, and put him back to bed.

A little group, including Lieutenant Keen, were leaning on the rails of the *Voltaire*, watching the attack with great interest – it was their first air raid and the barrage seemed to them fairly impressive. They saw the *Iron Duke* half hidden, time and again, by huge burses of white spray; they saw her heel over increasingly and begin to sink by the stern; with a slightly selfconscious air of bravado and superior knowledge they began to compare the list she was now taking on with a similar stage in the sinking of the *Royal Oak*.

Booth was in the *Iron Duke*, at first on her quarter-deck and then, when the buzzers sounded the alarm, down below under 'X' turret with a cup of rum given him by a Chief Stoker whom he had known in the light-cruiser *Durban*. There were two violent detonations, the main steam pipe cracked, bits fell off all over the place, the deck was obscured by steam, water began to come in, and the ship took on that familiar, increasing list. Booth was straight up on deck within seconds, asked permission to abandon ship, and went straight over the side, hanging on to his mailbag.

As he swam away, more planes were coming in at the *Iron Duke*, which was heeling right over to port, her guns still firing. Booth saw a gun crew fall away from a gun, after another bomb explosion; he saw a Marine run to an abandoned pom-pom and open fire. Bullets lashed the water among the swimmers – he was not the only one to have abandoned ship – and some of them disappeared in the old, familiar manner. Bombs were scattering the sea around the *Saint Abba* – he saw her go over and then come back again, apparently undamaged. Within minutes a fishing boat picked him up, the crew gave him a sheepskin coat, and then set him on the shore at Lyness, a few hundred yards away. He set off away from the Flow, carrying the sodden bag of mail.

Lieutenant Benton, in charge of a boat from the *Voltaire*, put away to pick up survivors from the *Iron Duke*; and swarms of small craft, virtually everything afloat in the area, began to converge on her. Acting as tugs, they closed the heeling battleship and began to push and pull at her sides with the object of beaching her before she sank. The bombers were still coming, and every gun that would fire was blazing away, even the colliers joined in. The fire was ragged, inaccurate and highly dangerous to all concerned, friend and foe alike.

From the deck of the *Voltaire* Saltmarsh was gazing fascinated at the big bombers diving down through the bursting black puffs of AA fire, the black crosses visible on wings and fuselage, and at the fountains of water shooting up from the Flow and then subsiding again. He saw the *Iron Duke* heel over amid columns of spray, and as the mailbags rolled off her deck a terrific roar of disappointment came from the rest of the *Royal Oak*'s survivors.

He saw one plane pull away from a bombing run on the battleship, the target of every gun that would bear. It suddenly fell away towards the interior of Hoy and went down behind a hill. Instantly a pillar of black smoke billowed up from the spot. Then, looking upwards, he could see a parachute, tiny and white in the distance, drifting imperceptibly downwards – there was a roar of cheering from the decks of the *Voltaire*. Slowly, the red sparks of tracer bullets began to climb up towards the man hanging under the parachute, and there was another savage cheer from the *Voltaire*; Saltmarsh felt sick.

The Fleet minesweeper *Hebe* claimed to have hit the aircraft with a three-inch 'brick'; a boom defence vessel commanded by an officer known as the 'Purple Emperor' claimed it, too; no one could really tell. But it was down all right, falling directly ahead of Sergeant Booch, crudging inland with his sodden mailbag. Having 'seen enough carnage already,' he altered course at once, and ran straight into the arms of a naval patrol sent out to bring in any surviving aircrew. What they saw was a man dressed in blue overalls, with a sheepskin coat which looked like a pilot's, trudging away from the scene of the crash.

They closed in on Booth and began to march him, under guard, back to Lyness. Booth, having just made his second 'ditching' from a sinking battleship, was not especially coherent. It was not until after several minutes' interrogation at Lyness that the Navy regretfully decided he was 'one of ours,' and put him into the *Iron Duke*'s cutter, still holding the mailbag.

By now the aircraft were flying back across the Pentland Firth and the *Iron Duke*, badly holed below the waterline by two near-misses, was steadily being pushed by the horde of small craft towards the northern shore of Longhope, a few hundred yards away. Pumps were quite unable to control the water pouring into her and she went to the bottom at last, technically 'sunk,' but upright in the shallows. And there she remained, with a concrete bottom and the water pumped out, for the rest of the war, still acting as depot ship.

A new patient was brought out to the *Saint Abba* – the German who had come down by parachute, the only survivor from the aircraft. As often happens in these cases with the best will in the world, the machine-gunners had missed him. He was suffering from burns and broken ribs.

In case of further raids, the Captain of the *Voltaire* cleared lower deck of all *Royal Oak* survivors; they were taken in boats to the island of Flotta, a few hundred yards away, and told to scatter. Their dinner would be brought to them. Lieutenant Benton came back from returning *Iron Duke* survivors to the *Iron Duke*, to be pressed at once into this service. He was returning from his final trip, closely followed by another boat of which Sergeant McLaverty was in charge, when air raid warning 'Red' sounded again. 'Christ,' he thought, 'I know what that means – the bar's going to close.' And it did.

'It was a fascinating experience,' said Leading Telegraphist Jones, 'to watch the Ju 88 squadrons come over in groups of nine at 12,000 feet in a bright blue sky. We could hear their engines long in advance, it was so quiet. We could see the bombs leave the aircraft in sticks and see the ships being straddled.' Batterbury was able to resist the fascination of the spectacle sufficiently to put his head down in the heather, out of the way of the splinters flying about. When he found that the heather was not heather, but the decomposing intestines of a long-dead sheep, he still kept it there.

'It was beautiful bombing,' said Lieutenant Keen, 'but the luck was dead against them.' A destroyer began to get under way and, as she gathered speed, a stick landed where she had been; another stick straddled the *Saint Abba*, another landed between the *Voltaire* and a collier, yet another straddled the boom. McLaverty's boat ran right into the stick aimed for the *Voltaire* and a water-spout leapt up a few hundred yards away. He let go of the tiller and the four rowers dropped the oars, while they lay flat; when they popped their heads up again, they had lost their means of locomotion and steerage until the '*Green Parrot*,' the Admiral's barge from the *Iron Duke*, took them in tow.

The battleship's cutter, in all this, was still heading for Flotta with Sergeant Booth and his mailbag; he saw cascades of water shoot up all round the boom and had the impression that one of the bar boats virtually became airborne, the waterspouts leading inexorably to the cutter. 'For Christ's sake. Coxswain,' he yelled, 'alter course, they're coming right for us!'

'Who's Coxswain?' replied the Coxswain.

On that, the next stick came whining down and Booth went through the air, still clutching the mailbag, for his third 'ditching' in four days. He swam the rest of the way to Flotta. As he crawled out of the water he met

Captain Benn, who said, 'What – not you, too?'

The German unit concerned in these two attacks was the Hinkelbein *Gruppe* of the Adler *Geschwader*, led by Lieutenant-Colonel Loebel. A *Gruppe* was roughly equivalent to an RAF Wing, and consisted of forty bombers. They were not opposed by fighters, except some invisible aircraft sent up afterwards by excited pressmen. The low-performance Navy fighters could not intercept and there were no RAF fighters based anywhere near. The *Luftwaffe* publication, *'Adler Jahrbuch,'* claimed a 'deadly blow.' It was hardly that, although they had certainly inflicted far more damage than they had received; they had also done far better than had Bomber Command in its attacks on German warships more heavily defended by flak, which was hardly surprising. The Intelligence 'tip-off' that an air attack on Scapa Flow was impending had been proved correct; their estimate of the numbers which would be involved had been locally wrong, their figure should have been divided by twenty. But the most surprising thing was that the *Luftwaffe*, like the RAF, were trying to sink warships by throwing tiddlywinks at them some fifteen years after 'Billy' Mitchell, to the fury of the US Navy and his own professional ruin, had smuggled 4,000-lb bombs into his aircraft and promptly put target warships of the same vintage as the *Iron Duke* on the bottom. It was not until Pearl Harbour that the advocates of the aeroplane came into their own.

The bombing did achieve one definite thing, however – it got the survivors home quickly. Captain Benn was heard speaking on the telephone in the *Voltaire*, apparently laying down the law to the Admiralty, insisting that his men had had enough of it, and had to be taken away. Just before dark they were taken off Flotta by the mine-sweepers *Hebe* and *Britomart*, and disembarked at Scrabster, the port of Thurso, about 6 p.m.; and after dark the *Saint Abba* got under way for Invergordon.

At least two survivors were better dressed in consequence. Paymaster Commander Cundall, in the hospital ship, was loaned a complete uniform by the Padre, who would not, however, include a collar in the loan. In the *Hebe*, Batterbury was given a pair of sailor's trousers with the right leg missing, an improvement on what he was wearing. McLaverty was still stuck with overalls and two left boots, 'big, gravel-punching Marine's boots.'

They were taken into Thurso and billetted, at very short notice indeed, in the homes of many kindly people. Mrs B Gunn opened the door of her house, that dark winter's night, to see two men there, one of whom was Stanley Saltmarsh. 'Stanley,' she said, 'was shivering in an old raincoat, vest and pants, with a pair of sandals on his feet. The other man was more decently clad, but the supply had run down. Stanley was violently sick and sort of delirious owing to the oil he had swallowed in the sea. Next morning I got grey pants and a pullover off my son and a brother-in-law supplied a warm jacket. Stanley has never forgotten and I still get a card from him at Christmas.'

None of the other survivors forgot, either. 'They stripped their wardrobes for us,' was the general comment. Booth, who had no shoes, was given slippers, plus a pair of fisherman's trousers and a tam-o-shanter, or 'balmoral.' One man, before leaving, was given a cake for the journey home, and found a ten shilling note underneath it. The way they were looked after by the Port Commander, known to them only as 'Peg-Leg Joe,' matched that of the inhabitants; 'He was a real gentleman,' said Parham.

Petty Officer Kennedy, Acting/Petty Officer Blundell, Able Seaman Ayles, and another man, were billetted together. They settled down, after food, to listen to the radio. As was normal in Britain at that time they tuned in to the enemy for light relief and diversion from the *BBC*. At 9.15, said Blundell, they heard a man announced as Lieutenant Günther Prien. He spoke in English. His U-boat had that day returned to Germany, after entering Scapa Flow, sinking the *Royal Oak* and damaging the *Repulse*. 'He spoke from Kiel,' recalled Blundell. 'He didn't give any details of how he got into the Flow. He said he could clearly see a battleship and a two-funnelled battle-cruiser, clearly silhouetted against the bright moonlit sky. And, although he spoke for five or ten minutes, that sentence was the only one that sticks out in my mind. I remember Kennedy and I looking at one another and saying, 'The ruddy liar.'

'It was pitch-black and cloudy; he couldn't have seen us from the distance he said he fired. As cox of the picket boat, I know that. There was a two-funnelled battle-cruiser near us in the morning, at the time the reconnaissance plane came over; the Germans wouldn't know that it left harbour a few hours later. The U-boat story was cooked; it wasn't there.'

CHAPTER TWELVE

'BLIMEY, WHERE'S SNOW WHITE?'

The sinking of the *Royal Oak*, as yet by 'an unknown agency,' on the 14th, the damaging of the *Southampton* and *Mohawk* by air attack in the Firth of Forth on the 16th, the technical 'sinking' of the *Iron Duke* in the first of the two Scapa air raids on the 17th, as well as previous attempts to lure warships into bomber and U-boat traps, made it clear that the Home Fleet was the target of a planned campaign designed to achieve by degrees what the Japanese were later to visit on the US Navy in one overwhelming blow. Clearly, further attacks were imminent.

The First Lord of the Admiralty (Winston Churchill) reacted with characteristic sweep and vigour; on the 18th he reported to the Cabinet that Scapa Flow must be for the moment abandoned as a fleet anchorage and decided that Loch Ewe on the West Coast of Scotland, which was hardly defended at all, would be the alternative base. In so doing he reacted exactly as the shrewd Germans anticipated and went straight into the trap, liberally scudded with magnetic mines, which they proceeded to lay for him.

He did not get his way without protest because, to anyone not obsessed with doing something regardless, even Scapa seemed better than Loch Ewe; and Rosyth, too, was vulnerable to mines. If the *Royal Oak* had been sunk by a U-boat the measures required were small – a few more requisitioned fishing drifters to patrol the entrances, or some lengths of cable, or a better watch, or a few small-calibre guns; if she had been sunk by explosives placed in the scores then the searching of scores before they were loaded would suffice (the survivors heard at Thurso that this was being done). But the last attack had been air attack and, although only forty bombers had appeared instead of the 800 predicted, it was air attack which loomed largest. The simple thought that the Germans might ring the changes, to keep everyone on the hop, was not sufficiently considered.

Ring the changes they did, by air and sea mining; and the results were soon apparent. On 21st November the brand new cruiser *Belfast* became a total loss in the Firth of Forth and on 4th December the battleship *Nelson*, flagship of Admiral Forbes, had an eighty-foot hole torn in her bows by a mine laid in the entrance to Loch Ewe. The losses were mounting, although some were kept secret. The *Nelson* went to Portsmouth for repairs and the Germans got wind of it. The Admiralty hate telling a lie and will go to great lengths of grammatical ingenuity to avoid doing so. They did not deny the German claim, they merely said that it was 'too ridiculous to deny.'

At Thurso, the Court of Enquiry into the sinking of the *Royal Oak* had begun on 18th October. Forms were handed out to all survivors, with a standard set of questions to be answered: (a) where were you at the time of the first – second – third – fourth explosions? (b) how many explosions did you hear? (c) did you see any flash, fire, smoke? (d) how did you get away? (e) who else was with you?

The results of these enquiries – diving operations and inspection of the entrances still continued – were never publicly divulged. Captain Roskill, the official historian, later skated delicately and with apparent naïveté over the whole question in two revealing sencences:

Meanwhile inside the Flow it was realised that a U-boat had probably penetrated the defences, but a search by every available vessel revealed no trace of her.

Such doubts as might still remain were dispelled a few days later when the enemy announced Prien's success ....'[1]

The onus of publicly stating that it was a U-boat was thrown onto the narrow shoulders of Dr Goebbels; his word was accepted without question, although he was gleefully capable of faking a U-boat into Scapa Flow and faking it out again and had, within hours of the sinking, kindly been given the hint by the Admiralty through *BBC* announcements.

[1] 'The War at Sea' Vol. I. by Captain S W Roskill. DSC.

Indeed, it was only a few weeks since he had faked a Polish attack on a German frontier post, complete with real, bullet-riddled corpses for the edification of newspapermen. In fact, the Admiralty were keeping an open mind on what had sunk the *Royal Oak*, but the German claim was a gift from the gods, as far as morale was concerned.

Among the survivors there was great relief at the news; many of them accepted it completely. Leading Telegraphist Jones cynically observed that if the defences of Scapa were anything like the rest of the war effort, any U-boat could get in any time it wanted. Which was perfectly true. Other survivors were spending their evenings in pubs trying to work out, with local skippers, whether a U-boat could get in and out again in the time allowed, and then return to Germany in time for Prien to broadcast from Kiel. The broadcast, which was reported in the British press on the 19th, hardly inspired confidence. It was pre-recorded and the following extracts were published:

> It was quite a job to smuggle ourselves into Scapa Flow through all the British defences. I saw two British warships to the north of me, and discharged two torpedoes at them. I at once turned my boat and left the harbour, because I did not want my ship and crew to be captured. As I left the port I heard two explosions and saw a column of water rising from the British ship lying farthest north. A moment later the other ship exploded.
>
> I saw parts of her blown into the air and then the whole ship disappeared. Then I realised that the northern ship was seriously damaged too – she had two funnels, which proves she was not the *Royal Oak*. Just as we were leaving the port intense activity began there. The surface of the sea was lit by searchlights, and several depth charges exploded behind us. You cannot imagine how cheerful and happy I felt when, a few minutes later, a thundering cheer sounded over the sea from my crew.

Prien gave a press conference, which was also reported in the British press. He told much the same amazing story as before, with the following additions:

> I saw straight in front of me the outline of two large warships. The first torpedo struck the boat with two funnels, which was the further away of the two vessels.
>
> The second torpedo struck the ship lying nearer to us.

As this partly screened the further ship, our first torpedo could only be aimed at the visible portion. It therefore struck the ship forward, as a result of which the vessel – I am speaking of the *Repulse* – was considerably damaged, the bows, as we established beyond dispute, sinking deep into the water. The effect of the second torpedo was queer. Several columns of water rose high from the ship's sides, and columns of fire were visible in all the colours of the rainbow. Bits of wreckage were hurled through the air. They were fragments of the tunnel, masts, and bridge. It was my aim not only to sink a British ship in a British Naval harbour, but also to keep my crew and boat for further tasks. We went out the same way as we had come in. Behind us great activity with searchlights and Morse signalling began.

As a result of this farrago of nonsense, the Germans were claiming that the *Repulse* had been damaged, as well as the *Royal Oak* sunk. When Petty Officer Kerr was sufficiently recovered to read these accounts he wrote in a scrapbook he was keeping of the affair:

Although the fifteen of us in hospital with multiple burns curse the U-boat for sinking our ship and killing 800 of our shipmates, we all say it was a courageous feat of seamanship of remarkable skill and daring, also the captain of her was a hero and a gentleman. But the stories published by the German press (the two reports just quoted) are all false claims, which makes it seem that the U-boat crew that was decorated by Admiral Raeder was for propaganda purposes and they never saw the inside of Scapa.

Submarine commanders' reports frequently are very inaccurate, particularly as regards night operations, but Prien's account went far beyond what might reasonably be allowed. One cannot damage a ship which is not there, or mistake a single-funnelled ship for a two-funnelled one, or mistake west for north, or imagine nonexistent search-lights and depth-charges. On all counts bar one the story was a fake. There were those curious repeated references to his withdrawal from Scapa, as though he were somehow ashamed of it.

Certainly the Admiralty were not taking it for gospel, although they affected to do so. A proportion only of the survivors were interviewed, after the forms had been checked; many of them must have been unsatisfactory. The men were fed up and, literally, far from home; they wanted to get away on leave. Others were intimidated by the array of rank, said 'Yessir' and 'Nosir' where required, and got out thankfully. Others again found that both fire and flash were frowned upon, the interviewers seemed to want not to believe it. Chief ERA Wilson, who had boldly written 'Internal explosions' on his form, was told, shortly, 'Tripe.' When Able Seaman Farley got in, they unbent sufficiently to argue the point. A torpedo, it was pointed out to him. Gravelled at some speed and might reasonably be expected to penetrate the hull before exploding. Farley said, afterwards, 'I didn't wear that.'

What that speed would be was a matter entirely of conjecture, unless or until sufficient fragments were found to reconstruct it. Twenty-six knots would be the probable speed, but there were rumours of German torpedoes of the trackless type capable of fifty knots, though they would not have said as much to Farley. On the other hand Stoker Cleverley, if he had been there, could have testified that the third explosion lifted the armoured deck in the cross-passage between the messdecks, almost on the centre line of the ship. That presupposed a torpedo sufficiently fast and a warhead sufficiently powerful to penetrate both the anti-torpedo bulges and several small compartments and then blow open the armoured deck, designed to keep out bombs and plunging fire from big guns, and so put Cleverley in hospital for nearly four weeks with flash burns. It really was a bit hard to believe. But if a container about the size of a torpedo warhead had been introduced into the central stores, which were somewhat on the starboard side but inboard, approximately where that explosion seemed to have occurred, then it would have produced just those results which had been brought so violently to Cleverley's notice. Additionally, Finley who was at the time directly above that point, but several decks higher, had been cut down at the precise moment of the third explosion by what appeared to be the flash from it. Unlike those aft of the Stokers' messdecks, who had been burned by an unmistakable cordite flame venting near the night 'heads,' Finley had been hit by an almost instantaneous flash travelling upwards, as the nature of his injuries indicated.

The Germans were suspected to possess, although there was no proof of its use so far, a magnetic fuse for use with torpedoes (technically known as a 'non-contact pistol'). Instead of striking the protected sides of a major warship, it would be set to run deep and explode directly under the hull, the most vulnerable point of all. Such an explosion would be unlikely to produce a waterspout and probably would give the impression of being internal; but it was unlikely to be used in the shallow waters of an anchorage. It is doubtful if it would have produced the results seen by Cleverley and it could not have cut down Finley.

When Leading Supply Assiscant Sims was interviewed, the word 'tripe' was not used in connection wich his belief that the explosions had been internal; far from it. The interviewers were most interested in anyone who could tell them precisely what had been put into the storerooms on the previous day; indeed he was a 'key' witness. 'It was a long interview,' recalled Sims, 'awkward questions, all about storing ship – the packages, how packed, anything suspicious. They thought there might have been a bomb planted in the food.'

Sims did not think so. He replied that the containers were mostly about $2\frac{1}{2}$ x $1\frac{1}{2}$ x $1\frac{1}{2}$ feet, weighing perhaps $\frac{1}{2}$ cwt. The bomb could not possibly have come in the guise of victuals; the packages were too small and too light. His suspicions of sabotage were based on the muffled nature of the explosions, as they had seemed to him, and the strange gaps between them; he had no idea where they had occurred.

On the other hand Sergeant Booth, who had been in charge of the Marine working party helping with the scores, recalled that five forty-gallon drums of oil had been loaded from a lighter cowed alongside by the *Daisy*. They were certainly heavy, he had lifted one, and they were about the size of a torpedo warhead. One he thought had been scowed forward in the CO_2 flat, near the inflammable store, three had gone into the central stores amid-ships, and the last had been scowed in the after tiller flat. In other words, more or less exactly where the explosions had occurred.

But if the explosions had in fact been sabotage that postulated a quite elaborate effort on the part of some person or persons unknown, which was disturbing to think about. In the first world war the Germans had destroyed quite a number of ships sailing from American ports by placing time bombs in them; but these were merchant ships and the bombs were really incendiaries. Placed in the cargo by an agent acting as a stevedore, they set fire to it, and that was that; quite a small bomb would do the trick. To destroy a 39,000 ton battleship by explosion was a totally different matter.

In a major warship, a small bomb would work only if introduced into a magazine; the magazines were the best guarded parts of the ship and two of the explosions, at least, had been nowhere near a magazine. Besides a magazine explosion would be likely to set off a shellroom and that would destroy the ship almost instantaneously, would produce in fact a second *Vanguard*. Prien's description of the sinking – 'fragments of the funnel, mast and bridge... hurled through the air' – although, curiously enough, having a more than passable likeness to the *Vanguard* affair, bore no relation whatever to the sinking of the *Royal Oak*. No main magazine had exploded, still less a shellroom, although some magazine, and that probably small, had vented and produced a cordite flame. As the divers were now finding out, the only magazine which had been wrecked, possibly by explosion, was a small-arms magazine.

A considerable quantity of high explosive must have been put in the ship, disguised as stores; furthermore, it could not have been added casually to the other stores as a surplus item, or there would have been questions from the supply staff. If it had been in the oil drums, then the drums must have been carefully prepared, because a solid-sounding oil drum would at once excite suspicion. And, at some point, the four or five items of doctored stores must have been 'switched' for similar stores already on the invoices. Granted that that could have been done, the rest was easy; new stores would be opened last, and it was unlikely that anyone would touch them in the few hours that remained before the time mechanisms worked. Those mechanisms would not be clockwork; at that stage of the war they were likely to be acid, and doubly likely to be unreliable, producing awkward gaps between explosions quite unlike the ten or fifteen second intervals of a submarine putting over her helm to produce a torpedo 'spread.'

There would, too, have been plenty of advance warning of the scoring operation. Before the *Royal Oak* entered Scapa, stores would have been demanded from a large number of departments, so that a great many people would know that a worthwhile target, a battleship, was due to score on a given day; and the stores would be waiting for her when she arrived. It was common talk among the survivors that some of the stores had been lying unguarded for twenty-four hours on Lyness jetty, stencilled with the *Royal Oak*'s name.

The ideal agent would be a storeman but, if that could not be managed, an outsider could 'switch' stores quite easily, provided that he knew roughly what would be on the invoices each time; observation might suffice. Orkney, although a delightfully different spot for a brief summer holiday and of course 'home' to its inhabitants, produced in men condemned to serve there for a term of years with no known end, a lethargy not unlike the 'cafard.' Guard duty, all too often, was little more than a farce. Indeed, on an exercise, 'B' Company of 2nd Gordons marched undetected from Rack Wick on the west of Hoy to within 100 yards of a battery then covering the Graemsay blockships. The attack, signalled by a smoke bomb from a two-inch mortar fired direct into the battery position, went in in full daylight, the assault platoons reaching the guns before the gunners had even stumbled out of their huts.

Similarly, if it was necessary to land the considerable amount of high explosive required, in default of obtaining it from local sources, then the operation, though not without melodrama, was virtually without risk. On a sparsely populated island like Hoy there was a selection of suitable spots. Indeed, the small number of inhabitants would present the first, and by far the most serious, obstacle to any sabotage operation; the initial infiltration of the spy would be immensely tricky – the newcomer would stick out like a sore thumb.

Walter Schellenberg, in his memoirs, stated that a German spy was infiltrated into the Orkneys in the 1920s. If it was done at all, that was when it was done. It was in 1924 that E F Cox, of Cox & Danks, shipbreakers, decided to buy the German High Seas Fleet, lift the seventy-two ships involved, and break them up for scrap. This immense task took years and involved the arrival in Orkney of a number of outside workers, besides the divers. Most lived in a camp, but some settled in with the crofters, all within easy reach of the HQ, which was – at Lyness. The fanciful 'Watchmaker Spy of Kirkwall' stories have all ignored the fact that, although Kirkwall is the capital of Orkney, it is remote from the naval base, which is – at Lyness. Probably the authors did not know that; they just jumped to conclusions.

At Thurso, while some of the survivors intensively discussed what had sunk their ship, a good many did not bother their heads about it; they went to the pictures. Sergeant Booth did. The main feature was, 'The Submarine Menace.'

But, with all this buzz of heated talk going on, there arrived, in force, in Thurso – the press. All survivors were forthwith given strict security warnings – 'under no circumstances communicate with the press.' The number of explosions was secret, the *Pegasus* was secret, the *Voltaire* was secret – none of this was to be communicated even to relatives. The result was that the pressmen spent their time in pubs, plying survivors with drink, and getting in return very remarkable experiences of personal survival.

In consequence, none of the main facts ever leaked out.

It was years before it began to dawn on suspicious German naval writers that the *Repulse* had not been there at the material time – Prien had said so, therefore it was so – and as late as 1958 the self-appointed historian of the U-boats, Wolfgang Frank, could conjecture that the first torpedo had struck either the *Pegasus*, the *Royal Oak*, or the *Iron Duke*!

Late on Thursday, 19th October, the buzz went round that the leave train was raising steam. Sergeant Parham was still down on the list of witnesses from whom a detailed statement was required; at the last moment he was told to get on, they had enough evidence already. Eventually, only Captain Benn and Commander Nichols were left behind, to help with the Court of Enquiry. Lieutenant Benton had to give up a deerstalk, which had been laid on by Lady Sinclair – the officers were accommodated at the Air Minister's residence, and this was the least of the hospitality offered them.

The leave train looked as if it were peopled by brigands – there was hardly a complete uniform there. Overcoats, already on order from Rosyth, arrived just before the train started. Men walked down the carriages, dishing them out. 'How many in here? Four? Right, here you are!' And four overcoats sailed in, any size.

Farley huddled himself up in his overcoat and, after a stop at Stirling for coffee and cocoa from the WVS, tried to go to sleep. A reporter, Farley thought he was from 'The Daily Herald,' was playing cards with the other men in the compartment. The train gathered speed – then shuddered to a stop with a violent crash. With reflexes now much sharpened, the other survivors were through the window in a flash, followed by the reporter. Farley came out from under his overcoat in the corner, to see that the luggage rack had fallen, one end of the seat had collapsed, and, where the carriage door had been, a raw truck-load of pig-iron was staring him in the face. The reporter was travelling fast towards the nearest telephone, shouting out words that sounded like, 'Boy, oh, boy, what a scoop!' and pursued by Lieutenant-Commanders intent on stopping any more alarmist stories getting out.

They had been rammed, at slow speed, by a goods train; it just happened that Farley's compartment actually took the impact. After a delay, they got in motion again, reaching Glasgow about 9 a.m. on the Friday. A sausage-and-mash breakfast had been laid on at a restaurant opposite the station; as they marched across the road in their motley attire, a harsh chorus of jeers, boos and catcalls met them from a crowd which was beginning to gather.

As they marched back, after the meal, the same crowd burst into a roar of cheering. Word had spread that they were *Royal Oak* survivors, not German prisoners.

From Euston they were taken across to Waterloo. When the train ran through Portsmouth town station, on the last mile of the 700, they were flat out – 'worn to a frazzle, it was like a ghost train.' It went straight through to Unicorn sidings in the dockyard, from where they were taken to the RN Barracks – everything had been laid on for them; and those who lived locally could go home for what remained of the night, if they wanted. As Batterbury stepped out of the gates for the first time into a blacked-out Portsmouth, somebody rushed at him from the unexpected darkness and flung her arms round his neck; after a moment, he realised that it was his fiancee, Farley had a different reception. He was stopped by a newsreel cameraman who fitted him up with a wife and two kids for a touching reunion. He only had one child at the time, and the wife wasn't his either, but it looked all right.

The Marines were taken to Eastney Barracks, three officers and forty men. There were more than eighty missing faces. Any of the survivors who lived locally would be taken home by truck, provided they reported at the barracks next morning. 'Local' really meant Eastney and, at the most, Southsea. But they went further and further through the city, the driver scretching things more and more. He dropped the last man off at Porchester, miles outside Portsmouth. 'Where do you live, chum?' he asked Saltmarsh, who hadn't the heart to say it was Gosport, seven miles further on. He compromised on Fareham, and walked home five miles through the night.

Many of the wounded, however, were still many months from home. The worst cases, who were kept at Invergordon, still could not sleep at night; so they talked or sang in snatches to each other. The hospital was new, they were its first patients; some of the orderlies were miners. Fossey still has a card autographed by a doctor. Surgeon Lieutenant Bryan C Murless, RNVR, Sister Mary A Montgomery, and nurses Molly Davidson and Elizabeth Ferguson. What each man feared was permanent disfigurement; they were afraid of what they would see when the bandages round their heads came off. For some there was the additional fear that their limbs would be permanently crippled. Stoker Tate and Leading Seaman Instance were the two most serious cases out of the fifteen who were kept there; after a few days, Tate died.

Changing the bandages was agony, cries of 'Brutal bitch' rang round the ward whenever it was done (although, privately, they all thought the staff were magnificent). The doctor decided that the pain was too much for already weakened men to suffer – there was oil fuel in the burns – and he introduced a system of wetting the bandages in a large tray, which got them off with much less discomfort. Instance was the most difficult case, because he required an operation to replace the flesh burnt off his hands – the blazing cordite had attacked the raised portions more than anything else. After six weeks, a skin graft was made to his right hand, which was then strapped up on a rest resembling a miniature crane. It had to be left untouched for a week but, as the smell became worse, Instance swivelled it away from under his nose. The patient in the next bed, much offput, pushed it back.

At length, when the seven days had passed. Sister Montgomery placed screens round him before starting to take off the bandages; other curious burn-cases began to crowd round the screens, peering over the top. But as the layers of bandage came off, the odour became more and more distinct and the number of heads looking over the screens became fewer and fewer. After a while, there were none; finally, the Sister herself could stand it no longer and fled for a nip of brandy. When the hand was bared at last, it was just a horrible mass of pus. Instance tried to joke: ' Let me have a nip too – I've had to live with this thing.' At that point the doctor judged that Instance's morale was low – 'so it was,' said Instance – and sent for his wife to come up and join him. When she arrived, it was too late – the pus had gone and the hand was 'clean as a whistle.'

On 20th November Kerr, Dommett, Campbell, Thatcher, Hancock, Hearn and Bond were discharged. They took the train for Euston, still in their makeshift clothes, with not a shred of naval uniform between them. Kerr's burns had cleared up, except for his ears, which still looked a bit like 'the crackling off roasted pork,' and his hair, which was burnt away at the front and on top. As they passed through the barrier at Euston, they heard two soldiers call out, 'We're looking for seven sailors who're supposed to be on this train.'

Kerr spun round. 'That's us!'

The soldiers stood a moment, gazing. 'Blimey!' said one, 'where's Snow White?'

With two weeks to Christmas, Instance was alone in the ward. On Christmas Eve, he travelled south with his wife, unable to wear uniform and with his hands protected by special gloves. In the train were a number of servicemen and to make conversation one of them turned to Instance with, 'Been touring the Highlands?' Instance told him. At a halt on the long journey, he badly wanted a cup of tea, but there was a terrific scrum at the canteen, so that neither he nor his wife stood a chance of getting one. At length, a Sergeant appeared – holding two cups of tea. He was followed by a Marine – with two cups of tea. Bringing up the rear was a sailor – with two cups of tea. The same idea having occurred to all three independently, the cups of tea were at last laid in rows on the floor of the carriage.

Instance, in his recovery, showed the same inflexible determination which had enabled him to survive; although his right hand never did regain its full use, with the aid of one doctor, he got round the others, remained in the Navy and is today a Lieutenant. For some time afterwards he was not happy in ships, particularly at night, and, because his escape had been due to knowing the *Royal Sovereign* class inside out, he made it his business to be able to walk round the ship with his eyes shut. Bendell, who had been trapped below, took his own lesson to heart and slept on deck as much as he could, wearing a lanyard, a knife and a whistle. Other survivors of the *Royal Oak* did not survive the war. Cleverley saw Chief Stoker W H Aplin during the Norwegian campaign (they lived in the same road and knew each other well); they had a few hours talk before Aplin left in the destroyer *Acasta* for home; on the way he met the *Scharnhorst* and *Gneisnau*.

Boy Trewinnard was drafted to the armed merchant cruiser *Vandyke*, a sister ship of the *Voltaire*; in her was another *Royal Oak* survivor. Sick Berth PO William Brigden. The *Vandyke* also met her end in the Norwegian campaign, Trewinnard was taken prisoner and spent five years in German PoW camps, until he was freed by a Russian force led by a motorcycle and sidecar. Although he can now recall little at the *Royal Oak*, he can vividly remember the amazing spectacle of the Red Army advance, a mass of horses, carts, and men on foot mixed up with brand-new Lease-Lend American lorries.

The Court of Enquiry cannot have found any fault with Captain Benn, for he was afterwards given another ship, the cruiser *Fiji*; curiously enough, half-a-dozen *Royal Oak* survivors, including Boxall, were among her crew when she sailed with the Dakar expedition and Lieutenant Benton was in another ship of the convoy. He was looking directly at the *Fiji*, when he saw a white water column leap up her side – she had been torpedoed.

Lawrence was in the destroyer *Worcester* when she had her stern blown off by an eleven-inch shell from the *Scharnhorst*. Wilson 'ditched' once more, from a corvette; so did Blundell, from the *Ark Royal*; Leading Telegraphist Jones was in the cruiser *Birmingham* when she was either mined or torpedoed (it was never known which) off Benghazi. In fact, a good many, in one way or another, subsequently acquired substantial knowledge of marine explosions; and they were divided in their opinion. Some thought that a real torpedo felt nothing like what happened to the *Royal Oak*; others felt it was exactly the same sort of thing. The explanation was, of course, that it all depended on where you were in relation to the explosion.

By the end of the war Prien was dead, and so were Endrass and von Varendorff, his two executive officers, whose questioning might have helped to resolve the really remarkable discrepancies between what actually took place in Scapa Flow and what Prien said had happened. However, the log of U-47 was captured, along with almost all the files of the German Admiralty; this, far from clearing up the matter, increased the mystery. Prien's wartime statements and the autobiography[2] attributed to him might have been passed off as propaganda, but this was an official document and what is revealed was a mixture of the untrue, the incredible, and the impossible. On the one hand there were the survivors of the *Royal Oak* describing, as it were, a blizzard at the North Pole, and on the other hand the U-boat commander who was supposed to have sunk them talking about a Carnival in Venice. It was a fair deduction that they had not been to the same place.

---

[2] *U-Boat Commander* by Günther Prien, published by Cerberus Publishing in the *Fortunes of War* series.

CHAPTER THIRTEEN

'SUCH EXAGGERATIONS
AND INACCURACIES...'

Prien's story, when tried on the survivors of the *Royal Oak*, produced a simple, unanimous reaction: it was regarded as conclusive proof that he was not within twenty miles of Scapa Flow on the night in question. Some, like Kerr, thought that another U-boat commander had been substituted; others, like Blundell, assumed that it must be a careless cover story for a sabotage operation. It was not that the story was exaggerated or inaccurate in any way, but that it was totally and absolutely wrong; it was not boasting, it was not wishful thinking, it was not a highly sensitive imagination sharpened by danger; it had no contact with reality at any point. It was a fake.

Nevertheless, it is Prien's story which has prevailed, which has been told again and again by writers all over the world; not a word has been breathed against it, except to correct the claim to have hit the *Repulse*, even by British official and semi-official authors. Here by accident and there by design, the legend of the 'redoubeable Prien,' hero of Scapa Flow, has been put forward as the unchallengeable, authentic account of the operation.

Unquestionably, part of the reason for its acceptance is the fact that Prien and his two watch-keeping officers, Endrass and von Varendorff, are dead; otherwise the truth must have come out long ago. It is equally certain that in some quarters – and not in Germany only – there is a reasoned disposition to let dead submarine commanders lie.

Who was Prien? According to the Germans he was a Saxon whose family had been hard hit by the inflation of the twenties; he joined the Merchant Service as a seaman and eventually obtained a Master's ticket but not a ship. After a period in the labour camps he eventually joined the German Navy and painfully worked his way up again. In 1939, he was by no means the most experienced of the German submarine commanders.

After the war, one of the most brilliant of the surviving U-boat 'aces,' then visiting London, was asked in casual conversation if he had known Prien and what he thought of him. The German replied that he had known the man; and had disliked him. The basis of his dislike appeared to be that Prien had degraded himself, and by implication the German Navy also, by letting himself be used for propaganda. 'You don't write your own story,' he said. 'They write it for you – and make you look a bloody fool.' This particular U-boat commander was prepared to obey any order given by his superiors, but he would not cooperate with Dr Goebbels. That was beneath the dignity of an officer of the German Navy. This attitude was not uncommon in some German circles, in which Hitler was briefly dismissed as the 'parvenu.' They were prepared to fight for their country in time of war, to go out and the for it if necessary, but they were not prepared to be turned into part of a propaganda circus.

It was on this latter point that Prien parted company with them, because Prien was prepared to allow himself to be used; as a natural result of that compliance, he was launched, first upon his own country, and then upon the world, as Germany's supreme submarine hero. His comrades-in-arms were not deceived, and it is to be doubted if his superiors were, but that put no brake upon the growth of the legend, which his death cemented. Indeed, as is often the case, one falsehood fathered another, and even his death became clouded by rumour. It was whispered that he had not died at sea – sunk by HMS *Wolverine* in 1941 – but in a concentration camp or in a punishment battalion on the Russian front. And the Scapa Flow exploit became still further distorted, in the post-war period, by stories of a strange spy, a Swiss watch-maker of Kirkwall, who was supposed to have rowed out to the U-boat and showed Prien the way through the defences, even pointing out to him his target, 'the mighty *Royal Oak*, pride of the British Navy.'

What was Prien's story? There are a number of variants, and we must be clear what these are. First – in order of public appearance – were his broadcasts and press interviews, quoted earlier, which caused the real witnesses of Scapa Flow to dismiss him as an impostor. The same story, very much elaborated, was published in Germany during the summer of 1940; purporting to be the autobiography of Prien, it was titled 'I Sank the *Royal Oak.*'[1] From internal evidence, it appears to have been written by a radio writer, to whom no doubt Prien told his tale.

This 'autobiography' provides much of the source material for those authors, mainly German and American, who have written the more exciting of the monographs on Prien. In particular, Wolfgang Frank – a German Naval war correspondent who sailed with Prien on a later occasion – draws heavily on it for the description of the Scapa Flow operation contained in his two books about Prien.[2] So, too, do some of the American journalists who are concerned at least as much with the 'Watchmaker of Kirkwall' as with Prien.

The latest variant – considered in order of publication – is the actual log of U-47, to which some of the semi-official German writers appear to have been given access during the war. This document fell into Allied hands at the end of the war and was published, in translation, by the British Admiralty in 1948. The mass of material,[3] of which the log is a part only, is prefaced by a cautious note to the effect that the documents are not to be taken entirely at face value; they represent only what the German Admiralty was willing to have included in official records. Nevertheless, British official and semi-official accounts of the sinking of the *Royal Oak* are in fact based, in part, on this document.

There are some omissions: a few incidents which appear in the 'autobiography' are not to be found in the log. Apart from this, the log is absolutely damning; it is the same story, basically, but with the falsehoods made explicit. And it cannot be passed off as mere wartime propaganda. But, when examined, it comes apart in the hand. The log, too, is a fake.

Now, knowing in detail exactly what did happen in Scapa Flow, let us, so to speak, run Prien's story through the projector, remembering that accounts of night operations, particularly by submarines, are hardly ever accurate. The question to be asked at each point is not 'Is this true?' but 'Could an honest man reasonably make such a mistake?'

The log extracts printed in Brassey's begin on 12th October, when U-47 is lying submerged off the Orkneys. According to *Jane's* she was a

---

[1] In the English translation, published 1954. The German title was '*Mein Weg nach Scapa Flow,*'

[2] The first, subject to wartime censorship, appeared In English translation In 1954, '*Enemy Submarine*'. The second was published in Germany, 1958, as ' *Der Stier van Scape Flow.*'

[3] Published in Brassey's '*Naval Annual, 1948*' as '*The Führer Conferences on Naval Affairs.*'

medium-sized 'sea-going' boat of 500 tons, smaller than the ocean-going types, but larger chan the coastal 'canoes.' Two hundred and thirteen feet long, with a beam of twenty feet and a draught of thirteen feet, her speed was just over sixteen knots. She carried five 21-inch torpedo tubes, four at the bow, one at the stern, and a crew of more than thirty-five men. In the evening the boat surfaced and came in to the coast in order to get a 'fix.'

She was still waiting off the Orkneys next day, Friday the 13th. The log records:

'Wind NNE 3-4, light clouds, very clear night, northern lights on entire horizon.'

Skipper Gatt's account reads:

'Fine day, wind from the NE, light to moderate; took a big liberty party from Scapa Pier just as the sun set, and it was a lovely evening.'

There is no mention of northern lights and, on being specifically questioned. Skipper Gatt answered:

'It was a dark night with a clear atmosphere, and picket boat cox was right when he said visibility was about 250 yards from ship.'

In his account written the following year for *'The Orcadian,'* and referring to the time of the first explosion at 1.04, Gatt noted:

'We could see nothing, as it was dark.'

The survivors, with one exception, do not recall any northern lights: it remains in their memory as a dark but starlit night, with no moon; men could be seen walking about on deck, but only as shadows; the cliffs half-a-mile away were visible, because they were silhouetted against the lighter blackness of the sky. Apart from that, nothing else could be seen. Some recorded their impressions within a few weeks of the occurrence: Petty Officer Kerr wrote in his scrapbook of 'the black night' and Leading Telegraphist Jones told a reporter it was 'pitch dark.' Undoubtedly, Blundell, the picket boat cox, was correct – visibility, except where an object was silhouetted against the sky, was not more than 250 yards. Indeed, it would be impossible to navigate a picket boat – or a submarine – across Scapa Flow without using a compass and, even then, in order finally to locate the *Royal Oak*, the course would have to be corrected when fairly near her by a reference known to the picket boat cox – the radio masts on the hill behind her. These, because they were silhouetted against the sky, were visible when the *Royal Oak*, much nearer, was invisible.

The one survivor who does testify to northern lights was an important witness – Commander Nichols – but his description nevertheless tallies reasonably well with that of the others:

> It was a flat calm night with no moon but a fair aurora by which one could fairly easily see men moving about on deck and the outline of the land against the sky could be seen some six cables away on the starboard hand.

As a practical test, it should be remembered that Chief Stoker Lawrence said of the time he got out of the port and walked up to 'B' gun-deck:

> Commander Nichols was there; I recognised him by his voice only, for it was very dark.

Lawrence was only a few feet away from Nichols, because they were engaged in throwing overboard the 'church deals.'

The survivors' descriptions of a dark night cover the entire period from dusk until dawn; those who went on watch at 8 p.m. give exactly the same account as those who came on at midnight, and the watchkeepers include Cadet Owen, on AA watch halfway up the tripod and Leading Signalman Fossey on the flag-deck. It is just possible that, at some time fairly early in the evening, there may have been a faint display of northern lights; but it cannot have been much or everyone would have noticed it. Certainly, the Flow was not brilliantly lit up; indeed, quite the reverse – it would be perfectly easy to get lost inside it.

After the crew of U-47 had had a warm meal, Prien recorded:

> Set course for Holm Sound. Everything goes according to plan until 2307 when it is necessary to submerge on sighting a merchant ship just before Rose Ness. I cannot make out the ship on either of the periscopes, in spite of the very clear night and the bright lights.

If his statement about the visibility was correct, this might be puzzling; but, if it was a dark night, then it was perfectly understandable. At 2331 (11.31 p.m.) the U-boat surfaced again and entered Holm Sound. It was now $1\frac{1}{2}$ hours after high water, but the current was still flowing in. There were now two openings ahead of Prien – Kirk Sound on the starboard bow and Skerry Sound on the port bow; and, in spite of what he had said was good visibility, he promptly mistook the one for the other and had to be corrected by his navigator, not by visual means but by a dead-reckoning check:

At first I believe myself already in Kirk Sound... but the navigator, by means of dead-reckoning, states that the preparations are premature, while at the same time I realise my mistake... By altering course hard to starboard, the imminent danger is averted. A few minutes later. Kirk Sound is clearly visible.

Again, if the night was; as clear as he made out, the error seems strange; but if it was dark, it was an understandable happening. Prien said the light was very good.

...Kirk Sound is clearly visible. It is a very eerie sight. On land everything is dark, high in the sky are the flickering northern lights, so that the bay, surrounded by highish mountains, is directly lit from above. The blockships lie in the sound, ghostly as the wings of a theatre.

The log now describes in detail, with compass courses, the complicated manoeuvring round the blockships in which the submarine is realistically depicted as wallowing along, driven broadside in places by the currents, striking the 'cable' of a blockship and taking the ground. 'Difficult, rapid manoeuvring' is the phrase, which indeed it would most certainly be if he chose to enter with a 'following tide!' Then he is in Scapa Flow and the time is twenty-seven minutes after midnight:

It is disgustingly light. The whole bay is lit up.

Owen had just come off watch; to him it was 'a perfectly ordinary starlit night.' Fossey had been on the flag-deck for nearly half-an-hour:

I had become thoroughly awake and got my eyes accustomed. It was a dark night. I couldn't see the *Pegasus* (about two miles away). I could see the top of the cliffs near us – where it met the lighter black of the sky. There were no northern lights.

Prien, once inside the Flow, turned – so he says – sharply to port and explored the main fleet anchorage, but found it empty:

To the south of Cava there is nothing. I go farther in. To port I recognise the Hoxa Sound coastguard, to which in the next few minutes the boat must present itself as a target. In that event all would be lost; at present south of Cava no ships are to be seen, although visibility is extremely good.

Even allowing for the fact that any U-boat commander, in such circumstances, would probably feel himself to be more conspicuous than he really was, Prien's description of the brilliance of the night is a gross exaggeration. That it was so is made fairly clear by the chart which is published with the log. This shows the track of the U-boat, with all the courses marked in degrees; the implication being that U-47 was being navigated inside Scapa Flow by dead-reckoning and not by visual means. However, it is the chart, by its very precision, which tends to raise the gravest doubts as to whether Prien was ever in Scapa Flow at all.

Prien says that he now turned again to port, this time through 180°, completely reversing his course, and went off to inspect the north-eastern corner of the Flow, where the *Royal Oak* was lying:

> We proceed north by the coast. Two battleships are lying there at anchor, and further inshore, destroyers. Cruisers, not visible, therefore attack on the big fellows.

The chart, printed in *Brassey's* with the log, and reproduced time after time, in all good faith, by German naval writers, shows the two 'big fellows' lying more or less in the positions accually occupied by the *Royal Oak* and the *Repulse* a day or so before, close together, and heading approximately east, with their bows pointing to the nearest part of the coast. This is inexplicable. What Prien saw, if he was there at all, was a single battleship – for there was no *Repulse* and there were no destroyers – heading approximately north, with her bows to Kirkwall and her starboard side almost parallel to the nearest land. There is no doubt whatever about that.

Almost all the survivors recall it, the only difference of opinion being that some thought she had her stern to Kirkwall and her port side to the land, as indeed she would have had earlier in the evening, before the tide turned. Rear-Admiral Benn (her Captain), on being asked, said that he thought her heading was a little west of north, but that Captain Nichols (her Commander) would probably be more definite. Captain Nichols said:

> She was heading north and was anchored about two miles south of Kirkwall pier.

Skipper Gate gave her heading as Kirkwall – that is, a little east of north, and added that:

> At low tide on 14th October you could see the bilge of the *Royal Oak* above the water and she was lying in the same position.

Captain W R Fell, who was in charge of the 1951 Survey of the wreck, said that, to his recollection, her heading was west of north. Mr McKay remembered that the wreck was headed roughly to Kirkwall, and so did Sergeant McLaverty, who saw her very shortly afterwards. As the *Royal Oak* did not swing at all, but simply rolled over to starboard and sank, the heading of the wreck would give, to within a few degrees, the heading of the ship at the time. In order to establish this with absolute precision, two Admiralty departments likely to possess large-scale charts of Scapa Flow were asked for this apparently harmless piece of information; but it was not forthcoming. In the absence of it, we know that her heading was approximately north, with a leeway of perhaps 5° either way. Her heading, as given by Prien's chart, is not less than 85° out.

Commander Affleck-Graves, Flag Lieutenant in the *Royal Oak*, also had submarine experience; when he was asked to say what tolerance might be allowed to a submarine commander in these conditions – a night operation, carried out under severe strain – he replied that errors of up to 60° might be possible, but certainly no more than that.

Even if we grant that, the night being very dark, Prien lost himself completely inside the Flow, the error is still so great as to make his return to Kiel, at best, problematical. But the error is not merely great, it is fatal, because it throws out the whole attack plan of the U-boat as shown on the chart. There, U-47 is depicted as firing torpedo salvoes from two slightly different positions which are two miles from the starboard side of the *Royal Oak*, and the log inexorably bears this out:

'Attack on the big fellows. Distance apart, 3,000 metres.'

But torpedoes fired from those positions would have hit the *Royal Oak* up the stern. To conform with the actual heading of the *Royal Oak*, the attack plan has to be bodily shifted almost through a complete right-angle – at least 85°. It is then seen at a glance that U-47 fired both salvoes from a position 1½ miles *inland*.

The Admiralty are tactfully silent on this point. They print Prien's chart in Brassey's, but in the official history[4] the position of the *Royal Oak* is shown by a conventional wreck sign with no indication of its heading. There is no hint there that the log of U-47 is false in any of its main particulars; although the author, Captain Roskill, has recently 'picked a bone' with Dönitz, he leaves Prien severely alone.

Assuming, however, that Prien lost himself, steered east until he saw the cliffs, then turned north towards Kirkwall, and so came across the *Royal*

---

[4] *'The War at Sea,'* Vol. I. by Captain S W Roskill. DSC.

Oak, the errors are still hard to explain. The *Royal Oak* was only half a mile from the shore. Captain Nichols says the land was 'some six cables away on the starboard hand,' and the map printed with the official history shows that he was exactly right. It is, of course, easy enough to misjudge distance over water, especially at night; by itself, there would be nothing remarkable in that. But Prien, in order to fire at all, must have been very close to the shore, must have been able to see the outline of the cliffs against the sky, must, one would have thought, have been aware that he was firing at a target almost due west of him instead of almost due north.

But in his log, and elsewhere, he continually refers, to the 'southern ship 'and the 'northern ship.'

> Attack on the big fellows. Distance 3,000 metres. Estimated depth 7.5 metres. Impact firing. One torpedo fixed on the northern ship, two on the southern. After a good 3½ minutes, a torpedo detonates on the northern ship; of the other two nothing is to be seen. About!

It is possible that he was hypnotised by an aerial photograph showing the *Royal Oak* lying in her correct position with the *Repulse* to the north of her. What Prien says he saw is not what he did see, but it may have been what he expected to see. An aerial photograph taken shortly before would indeed have shown a southern and a northern ship, and they would have been the two ships he reported them to be. But, as the *Repulse* had gone, what he was now looking at was an eastern ship and a western ship. The eastern ship was the *Royal Oak* and the western ship was the *Pegasus*. From *this* position, but not from the position shown on the chart, there would be two ships almost overlapping each other, almost exactly as he described them.

Indeed, Captain Roskill states categorically that Prien did in fact mistake the *Pegasus* for the *Repulse*, and, additionally, mistook his first hit on the bows of the *Royal Oak* for a hit on the *Pegasus*. German naval writers, without any hard evidence at their disposal, have speculated about that first hit, conjecturing that it might have been on the bows of the *Royal Oak*, or on the *Pegasus*, or perhaps on the *Iron Duke*. Prien had claimed that it had been on the *Repulse* and, when speaking to the press, added 'The *Repulse* was considerably damaged, the bows, as we established beyond dispute, sinking deep into the water.' He identified her as the *Repulse* because she had two funnels, whereas the *Royal Oak* had one.

The *Iron Duke* had two funnels, but she was ten miles away behind an island; the *Pegasus* had one, but was not hit. There were no other ships there, not even the 'tankers sleeping at anchor' mentioned in Prien's autobiography.

However, when the facts are examined, it becomes clear that Prien never saw the *Pegasus* at all. The *Pegasus* was nearly two miles away from the *Royal Oak*, invisible in the darkness; she must have been a further half mile away from U-47. If she could not be seen from the closer and higher vantage point of the battleship, she most certainly could not be seen from a submarine's conning-tower. In any case, with her long spindly smoke stack right aft – the most distinctive ship in the Navy – she could not be mistaken for the battle-cruiser, which had two funnels amid-ships.

But the really damning fact is that she was a much smaller ship than the *Repulse* and that she was a much greater distance away from the *Royal Oak* than Prien said she was. What Prien reported – and showed on his chart – was two big ships lying moored very close together; what he was looking at was one big ship very near to him and a much smaller ship a great distance away.

The *Repulse* was 32,000 tons (36,800 full load) and nearly 800 feet long; the *Pegasus* was 6,900 tons and 366 feet long. Now, it is perfectly possible, granted that the silhouettes are similar, to mistake what is in fact a very large ship, far away, for what appears to be a small ship, fairly close. But the actual position was the exact reverse of this – a small ship, very far away, being mistaken for one of the largest warships in the world lying much nearer. It was rather like mistaking a baby down at the end of the garden path for a hulking great all-in wrestler standing on the doorstep. It simply was not possible.

The first salvo of three torpedoes was fired, according to the log, at 0116, this time being queried in pencil and 0058 suggested. The latter time is within about four minutes of being correct for the first explosion in the bows of the *Royal Oak* (allowing two-three minutes running time). One hit is claimed (on the *Repulse*); two torpedoes missed. Prien then went about and fired his stern tube, without effect. Three misses at point-blank range.

Early in the war, German torpedoes were defective, and possibly that is the explanation; but the missing torpedoes were never accounted for, and that has not been explained.

The strange gap between the first explosion in the bows of the *Royal Oak* and the three explosions, some twelve minutes later, which actually sank her is explained by what Prien says happened next. While cruising, around on the surface, he reloaded three bow tubes and fired a second salvo from a position not far from the first one at a time which he gives as 0121, queried to 0102? and with 0123 suggested in pencil. None of these are really right, but near enough, assuming that everyone was too occupied to note them down and that they were estimated later, as is often the practice.

During this interval, the *Royal Oak* had switched on a 20-inch signal projector from the flag-deck and Fossey was playing it on the water on the port side, to illuminate the pieces of wood and straw drifting back from the bow; a wardroom 'light-excluding ventilator' had fallen down and light was showing through. If Prien saw these, he does not say so; the projector was certainly on the side of the ship farthest from him. He goes on directly to describe the arrival of the second salvo:

> Three torpedoes from the bow. After three tense minutes comes the detonations in the nearer ship. There is a loud explosion, roar, and rumbling. Then come columns of water, followed by columns of fire, and splinters fly through the air.

Midshipman Pirie, who was on the quarter-deck at the time and saw the explosions, was indeed less than a hundred yards away, described this as 'a gross exaggeration.' It is no more than that and, by itself, would be not at all remarkable; such trigger-happy descriptions are part of human nature. But the log entry does not stand alone. It is amplified by Prien's most-categorical report to Dönitz, which had just been published:

> Three hits on *Royal Oak*. The ship blew up within a few seconds.[5]

This report makes official what previously could have been dismissed as wartime propaganda licence – the description in Prien's 'autobiography' of how the torpedo explosions were followed by the detonation of a 'munition magazine' which tore the ship apart, sent huge fragments flying through the air, and produced a wall of water which blotted out the sky, so that Prien thought he was looking into 'the gates of hell.' German naval writers have added that 'whole gun turrets' were blown into the air. The descriptions coincide with remarkable accuracy with what McLaverty and Pratt saw at Scapa Flow, in 1917, when the *Vanguard* was destroyed within seconds by internal explosion; but they do not have the least resemblance to the *Royal Oak*. Captain Fell, who commanded the 1951 Survey, recollected:

> We found no trace whatever of any magazine explosion, except a small arms magazine which was wrecked, possibly by explosion.

---

5 *The Dönitz Memoirs*, serialised in '*The Sunday Times*,' January, 1959, and published in England by Weidenfeld and Nicholson.

The possible explosion of some .303 rifle and machine-gun ammunition becomes, in Prien's report to his superior, the detonation of at lease one shellroom containing 208 15-inch shells. In fact, there was not even a firework display, except momentarily, when the cordite flame 'vented' into the open air; the internal fires were not visible from outside the ship, only from the quarter-deck, when looking forward through the screen doors. Even the messdecks which were swept by flash or flame lapsed almost instantly into a glowing darkness so that, as Stoker Cleverley said, 'everything was black and red.'

Nor did the *Royal Oak* sink within seconds, as Prien implies, and as she must have done if a shellroom had exploded. Skipper Gatt thought she took about seven minutes, a survivor friend of McLaverty timed it at nine minutes, and Captain Benn, who attended the Court of Enquiry, afterwards put on record his belief that it was ten minutes,[6] The official historian. Captain Roskill, stated thirteen minutes,[7] which is probably too much; but, when commenting on 'The Evasions of Dönitz,'[8] corrected the Prien report only in so far as it concerned the *Repulse*. He did not draw attention to the discrepancy between his own previously published figure of thirteen minutes and Prien's 'the ship blew up within a few seconds.'

One would expect such an event, if it had really happened, to wake up even so vast an anchorage as Scapa Flow; and the log of U-47 goes on to describe exactly that:

> The harbour springs to life. Destroyers are lit up, signalling starts on every side, and on land 200 metres away from me cars roar along the roads.

Midshipman (now Lieutenant) Pirie curtly dismissed this as 'A lie – it did NOT wake up the harbour.' Lieutenant (now Commander) Sclater was equally definite, but more polite: 'I hardly think that even under conditions of strain, the U-boat commander could have made a mistake aboue these points.' Indeed, we know that the only immediate reaction, after the *Royal Oak* had sunk, was that the *Daisy II* put two lights on her wheelhouse and lay scopped, waiting for the swimmers to reach her; and that, subsequently, it was not until after 4 pm. – more than two and a half hours later – that the arrival of the *Daisy* at her gangway alerted the *Pegasus* and she briefly directed a signal projector on the water. She had seen and heard nothing, nor had anyone else. By that time, according to the log, U-47 had been outside Scapa Flow for about two hours. There were, in short,

6   'The Orcadian,' 21st October, 1948.
7   'The War at Sea,' Vol. I.
8   'The Sunday Times,' 18th January, 1959.

no search-lights, no signalling, no destroyers, lie up or otherwise, and, it must be added, no car on that road '200 metres away' because, in fact, there was no road there. The nearest road was nearly three-quarters of a mile inland.

As far as these points are concerned, the log descriptions are not exaggerations; they are fiction.

Prien now decides to withdraw, giving four reasons, three of which are certainly false:

> A battleship has been sunk, a second damaged, and the other three torpedoes have gone to blazes. All the tubes are empty. I decide to withdraw, because:
>
> (1) With my periscopes I cannot conduct night attacks while submerged. (See experience on entering.)
> (2) On a bright night I cannot manoeuvre unobserved in a calm sea.
> (3) I must assume that I was observed by the driver of a car which stopped opposite us, turned round, and drove off towards Scapa at top speed.
> (4) Nor can I go farther north, for there, well hidden from my sight, lie the destroyers which were previously dimly distinguishable.
>
> 0128. At high speed both engines we withdraw. Everything is simple until we reach Skildaenoy (*sic*) Point.

Reason number 1 is probably correct, because it was in fact a dark night, which gives the lie to reason number 2. Reason number 3 is impossible, whether one takes the log position or the chart position (they contradict each other). According to the log he has just sunk the *Royal Oak* and is '200 metres away' from land – which he would in fact be, if he had attacked her from the only possible position from which hits could be obtained on her starboard side, At that point the cliffs, which some of the survivors had tried unsuccessfully to climb, would be high above him, absolutely excluding all view of the road which, according to him, must have been on the cliff top, but is in fact nearly three-quarters of a mile inland. However, according to his chart position, he is not there at all but two miles south and nearly two miles out from the shore, conducting a northward attack from a position NW of Skaildaquoy Point.

From this position he would have been more than two and a half miles from the road (A961 – Kirkwall to St Mary's). At that distance, on that night, a car would not have been visible. It must be remembered that, in those blackout days, the 'headlights' of a car were merely narrow slits, directed downwards at the road, produced by fitting hooded masks over the lamps.

Reason number 4 is interesting, because it suggests that, contrary to appearances so far, he really was in Scapa Flow – and it points to exactly where he was at the time and furthermore gives a possible clue to the reason for the faking of the log in so many major particulars. Number 4 reads:

> Nor can I go further north, for there, well hidden from my sight, lie the destroyers which were previously dimly distinguishable.

Disregarding the fact that the destroyers are fictitious, and charitably assuming that, at some point, he imagined he could see the drifters at Scapa Pier, despite the fact that no one in the *Royal Oak* could see them – or indeed, Scapa Pier – and that drifters which he could not see became, in his mind, destroyers which he could see, it is just possible that there is some truth in the tale. The implication is that he was not deciding to withdraw, but had already withdrawn and had rounded Skaildaquoy Point, from which position the cliffs and the scene of the sinking would no longer be visible. The impression is heightened by the fact that at *this* point he could indeed have seen a car.

Just east of Skaildaquoy Point, on the northern side of the channel, is the village of St Mary's; the road from Kirkwall leads directly down to the shore at this point and then follows it for a distance of about a mile. Prien – from here – could have looked right up the Kirkwall road and, where the channel narrows by the island of Lamb Holm to a width of barely half-a-mile, he would have been only quarter-of-a-mile away from any traffic. Mr Allan, who was then a Police Constable at Kirkwall, states:

> It is quite possible that a fair amount of traffic would have been about even at that early hour, as large numbers of troops were concentrated in that area, a great many of whom might have been recuming even then, from various functions in Kirkwall or surrounding districts. The statement that the driver of a car may have observed him, seems to me to be unlikely, although one still hears this tale, along with others (since proved false).[9] Car lights especially during this early period of the war

[9] One of these stories occurs in Churchill's '*The Gathering Storm*,' in what he calls 'an account based on a German report written at the time':
'A man on a bicycle could be seen going home along the coast road.'
This refers to the penetration, not the withdrawal, and, in view of the darkness of the night, is in the highest degree unlikely. Churchill's own description of the sinking is marred by an error quite extraordinary, considering that at the material time he was First Lord of the Admiralty:
'*Most of the men were at action stations,* but the rate at which the ship turned over made it almost impossible for anyone below to escape.' (*My Italics.*)
In fact, some of the survivors were rather bitter, because they had *not* been brought to action stations; the number on watch was actually about too out of more than 1,200.

were very strictly dimmed out. I don't think a car light would have picked her up.

This suggests strongly that Prien's four stated reasons for withdrawal were no such thing; they were excuses for withdrawal, thought out afterwards; and in order to make them more convincing events which happened later and in another place were described as if they had occurred at the time and place of the sinking. This, too, would explain at a stroke why it was 'disgustingly light,' why the *Royal Oak* exploded spectacularly like the *Vanguard*, why the harbour 'sprang to life,' and why there was an orgy of lights and signalling. If all this had been true, no one could possibly question the wisdom of immediate withdrawal; a submarine commander would have had no other choice. It does not, however, explain how U-47 came to be one and a half miles inland – that error of almost a right angle is still inexplicable.

Prien says that he withdrew at 0128 – and that is almost certainly correct; it is the time, approximately, when the *Royal Oak* rolled over. After rounding Skaildaquoy Point, he says:

> Then we have more trouble. It is now low tide, the current is against us. Engines at slow and dead slow, I attempt to get away. I must leave by the south through the narrows, because of the water. Things are again difficult. Course, 058, slow – 10 knots. I make no progress. At high I pass the southern blockship with nothing to spare. The helmsman does magnificently.
>
> High speed ahead both, three-quarter speed and full ahead all out. Free of the blockships – ahead a mole!
>
> Hard over and again about, and at 0215 we are once more outside. A pity that only one was destroyed.

There is something badly wrong here. But it cannot be checked by observation because Kirk Sound is now blocked by No. 1 Churchill Barrier, a causeway built by the late Mr Andrew Baillie Sharp. On so variable a matter as tides, only local, professional knowledge is of use. Skipper Gatt, who has made his living in these waters for the best part of his life, states:

> At high water in the Sound, the flood still runs nearly two hours after, so Prien could have entered the Sound when there was still some Flood

---

10 'Reed's Nautical Almanac, 1939,' edited by Captain O M Watts, FRAS. AINA, gives the Greenwich mean times of high water at Kirkwall as
Friday, 13th October ... ... 10.15 a.m. ... ... 10.27 p.m. (12.3 ft.)
Saturday, 14th October ... ... 10.51 a.m. ... ... 11.09 p.m. (13.0 ft.)

time, and did his job, and got away at Slack water or the first of Ebb.

Now, Prien certainly did enter while there was still some flood time. He noted 'following tide' – and that agrees with the tide tables.[10] High water at Kirkwall was at 10.27 p.m., so that high water in Kirk Sound would be at about 10.00 p.m. Prien entered at 11.31 p.m., with about half-an-hour of flood to go. And he goes out again, between 1.28 and 2.15 a.m., when it would be slack water or the beginning of the ebb, just as Gatt says. But what he describes is certainly not slack water and hardly the beginning of the ebb – he meets the tide coming in again at *ten knots* two hours after the end of the last flood tide.

This phenomenon, of the tide coming in at ten knots when it ought to have been going out at some lesser speed, is not readily to be explained by any desire to fool Dönitz. Indeed Dönitz states in his memoirs that the night of 13th/14th October was chosen because 'both periods of slack water would occur during the hours of darkness.'

He appears to have had in his mind, when planning, similar considerations to those expressed locally, when Mr Allan was good enough to make enquiries on the spot:

> Information I have obtained from a local retired Merchant Navy Captain is that Prien surely timed his entrance just before the tide turned, so that he would have the tide against him, on entering and leaving the Flow. One reason given was that having the tide against him, it made his approach to the narrow channel slower, thus enabling him to navigate easier. Had the tide been with him, the rush would probably have driven him on to the rocks, especially so, as it was a narrow channel. The tides at that particular spot were very strong indeed.

Dönitz, all through, appears to have had no apprehensions about there being sufficient depth of water; he was worried only about the actual navigation. This accords exactly with everything we know about Kirk Sound as it was in 1939. It is Prien – again – whose account casts doubt upon whether he ever in fact carried out the operation. There is, however, at planning level, one curious divergence from established face. One of the more thoughtful of the German naval writers, Harald Busch, who obviously had access to the planning documents, states that the operation was to take place on a rising tide, so that, if U-47 went aground, she would float off. Indeed, he says it did take place on a rising tide.[11] But it was, in

---

[11] 'U-boats at War' ('So war der U-boot Krieg').

fact, carried out on a falling tide, as a glance at the tide tables shows.

Before turning to the final entries in the log, it is necessary to consider a variant of this story of the withdrawal through Kirk Sound, which appears only in Prien's 'autobiography' – and, of course, in the accounts written by the semi-official German naval writers, who appear to accept the 'autobiography' as authentic. It is not in the log.

U-47, retreating, is held motionless in the grip of the ten-knot current. Both engines are flat out. Then, from the 'welter' of lights in Scapa Flow, the headlights of a destroyer appear, making direct for the U-boat. Prien has the electric motors coupled up. Now the destroyer is so near that they can see its 'narrow silhouette.' Then it begins signalling. At the very last moment, when it seems that they must have been discovered, the destroyer turns away and there comes 'the *weeyummm* of the first depth-charges.'

At this time – about 2 a.m. – the nearest vessel to U-47 was Skipper Gatt's *Daisy II*, lying stopped some three or four miles away, with a rope wrapped round her screw; and, as it happens, out of sight round Skaildaquoy Point. The two destroyers were lying behind the islands ten miles away, and did not move until dawn. There was no depth-charging of any kind. Silent as the log is on this point, it does nevertheless mention depth-charging later on:

> 0215. Set SE course for base. I still have five torpedoes for possible attacks on merchantmen.

> '0630. Lay submerged. The glow from Scapa is still visible for a long time. Apparently they are still dropping depth charges.

When Prien returned to Germany on 17th October, he reported to Dönitz:

> After leaving Holm Sound observed great anti-U-boat activity (with depth charges) in Scapa Flow. Was greatly bothered by brilliance of northern lights.'[2]

He had indeed good reason to say that, considering the log entry: '*I still have five torpedoes for possible attacks on merchantmen.*' If he was in fact in Scapa Flow, then he had been put there by Dönitz, after considerable trouble; a big success must have been expected, possibly two or three major warships torpedoed. To leave after torpedoing only one, and with the anchorage still asleep, might have been human but was hardly heroic. He did, of course, improve on his actual performance by claiming the *Repulse* also as a victim.

But was he ever there? It is very hard to say, because he was so

---

[12] The Dönitz Memoirs (Weidenfeld and Nicholson).

unscrupulous. A month later – in November, 1939 – he sank the 10,000 ton cruiser *Norfolk* east of the Shetlands. Once more, the log of U-47 was quite categorical, even to those small details which always add verisimilitude:

> I recognise a cruiser of the '*London*' class. Range 8 hm. (approx. 880 yards). One torpedo fired from No. 3 tube.
>
> After 1 min. 26 secs. an explosion heard. I can see the damage caused by the hit, aft of the funnel. The upper deck is buckled and torn. The starboard torpedo-tube mounting is twisted backwards over the ship side.
>
> The aircraft is resting on the tail unit. The cruiser appears to have a 5° list to starboard, as she disappears on a reciprocal course into a rain squall.[13]

So sank the *Norfolk*. When Prien reported her destruction, the German radio went wild at this second triumph by the hero of Scapa Flow. The *Norfolk* returned to harbour, undamaged, her crew under the impression that an aeroplane had dropped a bomb astern of them. The torpedo had in fact missed her completely and exploded on striking her wake. Dönitz, in due course, noted in his war diary:

> Following the report that U-47 had torpedoed a cruiser. Propaganda claimed a sinking. From the service-man's point of view such inaccuracies and exaggerations are undesirable.[14]

The fact that the log of U-47 is a fake in almost all major particulars, except for the date, is consequently no proof that Prien 'never saw the inside of Scapa,' as Petty Officer Kerr expressed it. On the other hand, if the Germans were looking at short notice for a U-boat commander who would be prepared to lend his name to a Goebbels propaganda stunt designed to take advantage of the British Admiralty's swift admission and to cover up a sabotage exploit, then Prien would have been exactly the sort of man they would have chosen. Indeed, the best proof that Prien did sink the *Royal Oak* comes from British sources.

---

[13] '*The Gathering Storm*' by Winston Churchill (Cassell). Appendix N.
[14] *Ibid.*, Appendix N.

CHAPTER FOURTEEN

THE WATCHMAKER WHO NEVER WAS

Before summarising the conflicting evidence on the question of torpedo or sabotage, it is necessary to get out of the way the most popular and widely published of all the Prien stories, 'The Watchmaker of Kirkwall.' It originated as an article, 'Der Mann, der die *Royal Oak* versenkte' ('Man Who Sank the *Royal Oak*'), published in '*Der Kurier*,' Berlin, on 24th December, 1947. So eye-catching was this story that it has continued to circulate, appearing in England as late as 1957, under the same tide, but attributed to Dana Prescott.[1] The original article was unsigned. In this, the first version, the log of U-47 (for what it is worth) plays no part; and there are some departures from Prien's 'autobiography.' And a new personality is introduced, the watchmaker of Kirkwall who is said to have made the whole thing possible.

His real name is Alfred Wehring, a distinguished German naval officer who had fought against the *Royal Oak* at Jutland; in the 1920s he is sent to Switzerland for three years to learn the trade of watchmaker and acquire a new name, Alfred Oertel; in 1927, as a Swiss watchmaker, he sets up in business at Kirkwall. A month after war begins, he learns that the defences of Kirk Sound are not complete and radios the news to Germany. A U-boat – the B-06 – commanded by Prien is ordered away from patrol to

---

[1] '*Everybody's*,' 16th March, 1957. (An extract from '*Rough Passage*,' Hutchinsons).

rendezvous with him at Holm Sound. Oertel is taken off in a rubber dinghy and personally navigates the B-06 through Kirk Sound. Once inside, he takes the U-boat to the main fleet anchorage, which is packed with battleships, cruisers and destroyers. 'Never before did Prien realise the magnitude of the British fleet.' But the watchmaker will have none of these, he takes Prien to the last ship in line, the *Royal Oak*, 'pride of the British Navy.' Prien then sinks her at once with two torpedoes. Oertel is taken back to Germany, and disappears in the crowds wildly acclaiming Prien.

The idea of a battleship which had fought at Jutland being 'the pride of the British Navy' twenty-three years later, when she would have been overdue for scrapping and replacement, is absurd; the watchmaker, too, in his many diverting details, is a child's vision of a spy. But there are some minor pieces of information and misinformation which are interesting.

The date of Wehring's visit to Switzerland coincides neatly with the beginning of salvage operations at Scapa Flow on the High Seas Fleet – a possible opening for a spy, not in the guise of watchmaker at Kirkwall but as a salvage technician or even labourer at Lyness. The curious designation for the U-boat – 'B-06' – might be worth investigating from the German side. The descriptions given of the *Royal Oak*'s armour protection make it appear that the author had looked at *Jane's* – and partly misread it. The *two* torpedoes which sank her instantly are a faithful reproduction of what Prien said in his first press and radio reports. And the unknown author does get one thing right – he says it was a dark night. He also gives the little-known snippet of information that the Orkney mainland is known as Pomona, but nevertheless says that Scapa has only two navigable entrances.

It seems possible he was a non-naval type, who had got wind of some sort of German intelligence work in the Orkneys, and, in the shattered, starving Germany of 1947, was unable to fill in his background correctly.

The second version of the story has been re-written so thoroughly as to rub out most even of these tiny clues. The log and the 'autobiography' have both been drawn on and subsequently 'married' to the watchmaker, by an author with some naval knowledge. The resulting story appeared as late as 1958.[2]

Both versions have caused untold annoyance to some German naval writers, who have carried out detective investigations in – of all places – Germany. None have risked apparently so much as a 40-pfennig stamp on

---

[2] '*The U-boat Mystery of Scapa Flow*,' by Bourke Wilkinson, which first appeared in the '*Saturday Evening Post*,' 8th January, 1949.

a letter to Kirkwall. Considering that enquiries there should either prove or disprove the story once and for all, this is strange.

If the story was untrue – and it is – local newspapers must before now have exposed it. Perhaps – Prien's own story being what it is – close contact with Kirkwall was felt to be undesirable.

An enquiry addressed to the Editor of '*The Orkney Herald*.' Mr Ernest W Marwick, showed that he had already investigated the 'Watchmaker' and found no trace of him. Among others, Mr Marwick contacted the leading jeweller and watchmaker in Orkney, Mr W Hourston, of 34, Albert Street, Kirkwall, who was good enough to supply a signed statement, dated 18th February, 1959:

> As a jeweller and watchmaker who has been in business in Kirkwall all my life, and as a citizen whose knowledge of Kirkwall throughout the years has been complete, I certify with the utmost assurance that never at any period has there been a watchmaker in Kirkwall known as Albert Oertel, or any person connected in any way with the trade who could possibly be identified with the mythical 'watchmaker of Kirkwall.' I am convinced beyond the possibility of doubt that such a person has never existed, and is only a journalist's fabrication.

The Department of the Chief of Naval Information, Whitehall, had already, on 20th October, 1958, stated:

> The story of the 'Watchmaker of Kirkwall' is a fairy tale.

The Germans also strongly deny the story, which makes it unanimous; apart from that, internal evidence, as we have seen, clearly shows it to be a concoction.

To prove or disprove sabotage – which would replace the mythical 'Watchmaker of Kirkwall' by a hypothetical 'Saboteur of Lyness' should have been similarly straightforward. But it proved, in fact, very hard indeed. Now, this may have been because the authorities were understandably sensitive about the *Royal Oak*; the testimony of the survivors shows; that the state of the Scapa defences was on par with that of the rest of the war effort at that time, the dire result of disarming at leisure and rearming in haste. The Prien story, showing a much higher state of preparedness than was in fact the case, was less painful than the facts; indeed, this might well explain why the official and semi-official histories accept so much of Prien's story which is demonstrably false, or at least refrain from pointing out where it is false. However, this is supposition. But sensitiveness there undoubtedly was, and great caution.

There were a number of ways of finding out the truth. The first was to obtain (1) a large-scale plan of the ship, showing exact locations of storerooms, and (2) a plan or model of the wreck, showing the location and extent of damage; then bring to the same scale and place one on top of the other. If the holes corresponded exactly with the storerooms – as so many survivors thought they did – then there would be no further doubt. It was sabotage. If they did not correspond with precision, then it was torpedo.

The existence, and even the exact location, of plans and a scale model of the wreck was soon verified; but no access to them could be gained. Requests for constructors' plans of the ship proved futile. There was therefore a certain amount of leeway in the sabotage story. Half-a-dozen of the survivors interviewed were Supply staff and could say approximately where the storerooms were; the number and location of the explosions was known, but, again, only approximately. The coincidence between storerooms and explosions pointed to sabotage, but it was far from being proof.

The second way was equally obvious, but more complicated than it appeared. Divers' reports, if thorough and comprehensive, would reveal whether or not the explosions had been internal or external. Stories were going round among survivors that certain named divers had told them either that the explosions were definitely internal or that the hull had been blown outwards, which was less definite. If the torpedoes had penetrated to any great extent the edges of the holes might well be blown outwards. But these divers were not willing to be interviewed and, to complicate matters, the Admiralty seated that 'the plating was blown inboard and the *extreme edges of hulls bent in*' (my italics). This was disconcerting, because it appeared to contradict the validity of the 'penetration' theory and to conflict wich certain evidence which showed that the third explosion was deep inside the ship. The civilian contractors who had supplied divers were unable to help; their reports were the property of the Admiralty. In short, the all important *independent* corroboration was missing.

The third way, also obvious, was to check on other stories – also current among survivors – that divers had found torpedo parts and, in particular, torpedo calls, in the vicinity of the wreck. But the mere fact of a diver finding parts of a 21-inch torpedo was by itself not good enough. The *Royal Oak* carried four 21-inch torpedo tubes in the bow. The first explosion was definitely known to have blown away part of the stern and keel; and it was perfectly possible that parts of British torpedoes were lying about down there. The parts had to be proved to have come from a German torpedo. The tantalising fact was that it was known also just where those torpedo parts had been taken for examination.

After some three months, the Admiralty produced their proof. And very good it was. It constitutes the best evidence by far that the *Royal Oak* was in fact torpedoed. The first five pieces of a recovered torpedo had been analysed in December, 1939; the metals appeared to be of a different composition to those used in British torpedoes. Very probably it was a foreign torpedo. Later, a great many parts of two torpedoes, including the tails, had been recovered; and reported on in January, 1940. Among the parts was the perfectly legible nameplace of a motor – the words 'Siemens-Schuckert' put the matter beyond reasonable doubt, without going farther. Most interesting of all was an estimate of the distance the torpedoes had in face run to their target. The conclusion was that that distance had almost certainly been less than a mile. That fitted the facts, even if it did not agree with Prien's log.

This evidence was, and apparently still is, secret; although that may be merely because it has not been reclassified. To fabricate it, although perfectly possible, would take a great deal of time and trouble and, failing a very strong motive indeed, is in the highest degree unlikely. In any case other than that of the *Royal Oak* it would be absolutely conclusive. But, starting with the log of U-47 and ending with the 'watchmaker of Kirkwall,' there have been so many strange fabrications connected with the sinking that what is required still is the testimony of a disinterested third party – namely, the divers who would not talk.

Perhaps that is not quite the right word – they talked all right, to survivors. It was because they had talked that it became possible to ask a certain Admiralty establishment for the specific evidence which, in due course, they produced. It was no random or general enquiry. It was known that torpedo parts had been recovered, and that chey included two tails; it was known who had recovered them and where they had been taken. Strictly speaking, this was hearsay, but it proved to be absolutely correct. If so, then the second-hand evidence of another diver, to the effect that the explosions were internal and the plates blown outwards might be equally correct. It leaves, in the circumstances, at the very least a nagging doubt.

The Admiralty case for torpedo rests only partly on the fragment?

recovered from Scapa Flow; they cite also the German documents. It is apparently believed that, as the Germans could not know that they were going to lose the war and that these documents would be captured, there was therefore no reason to fabricate, for instance, the log of U-47. But this will not stand a moment's scrutiny. The semi-official writers working on the Prien story during the war for patriotic propaganda purposes might well ask for access to the log; indeed, it seems they did in fact have access to it.

The only established case of the 'faking' of a U-boat's log by the German Admiralty was that of U-30, which sank the *Athenia*, contrary to instructions. The process was quite simple – the removal of an original page and the substitution for it of another. Here, there was no question of journalists ever wishing to see the log. The faking was done in order to keep the facts of the *Athenia* affair secret *within* the German Admiralty. Had the log not been doctored, then the facts would automatically have been entered in the War Diary. As there were eight copies of this, in the course of time a considerable number of officers would have known the truth. To avoid this, there was to be nothing on paper to prove that U-30 had anything to do with it. Additionally, Lieutenant Lemp and his crew were given a direct order to keep silence. They obeyed.

Presumably the crew of U-47 would have done the same. It should be noted that the order to 'doctor' the log came direct from the Government, because the Propaganda Minister had already denied that a U-boat had sunk the *Athenia* and was not prepared to retract. It should be noted also that the matter came to light in the end only because the most immense and extraordinary pressure was applied. Germany not only lost the war, but was occupied; she was to be 'reeducated' and 'all vestiges of militarism' destroyed. For this purpose, as many military and naval leaders as possible were to be brought before the Nuremberg Tribunal, convicted, and hanged. In these circumstances, the truth about the *Athenia* became known. But no one was interested in the *Royal Oak*, and no such intensive pressure was applied there.

In short, fabrications of this order require Government action and a strong motive; the same requirements generally hold good if the fabrication is to be exposed.

There is no known reason why any politician should wish to 'hush up' the facts of the *Royal Oak* sinking and, furthermore, actually to manufacture very detailed evidence for the presence of a U-boat, evidence which anyway was in the 'Secret' category. The latter is the more important point because, as we know, there was very good reason at the time to hope that the *Royal Oak* had in fact been sunk by a U-boat; and the German announcement of Prien's exploit did vastly improve morale. It can hardly have been thought that it was necessary to show the torpedo parts privately to senior officers; although, in at lease one case, this was actually done – but merely as a matter of interest.

It must then be regarded as virtually certain that Prien did in fact torpedo the *Royal Oak*, although not in the manner he described. Most of the inaccuracies in his official reports may be hypothetically explained. The first 'hit' on the *Repulse* may have been a genuine error (because the night was dark and Prien could not perhaps clearly make out even the *Royal Oak*), or it may possibly have been a deliberate invention (consider the *Norfolk*); the northern lights, the *Royal Oak* blowing up in a few seconds, the subsequent orgy of searchlights, signalling, car headlights, and depth-charging may have been invented as an excuse for retiring from the enemy's main fleet anchorage with five torpedoes unused. Other equally imaginary incidents may be assigned perhaps to wartime propaganda licence. Even so, it is a truly formidable total of major discrepancies.

But this list is still not complete; there are other discrepancies for which there is no apparent explanation – except that, simply, Prien was not there. The most startling of these are the log references to 'southern ship' and 'northern ship' as a description of what were in fact an eastern ship and a western ship, taken together with the chart, which shows these two ships heading due east instead of, as was in fact the case, almost due north. A possibly erratic compass will not explain this, because the lie of the cliffs must have been visible, and they ran nearly north-west, providing a roughly accurate guide to direction; equally certainly, Prien cannot greatly have mistaken his position, for he shows the *Royal Oak* not very far from where she actually was. The error involves not only a fantastic mistake in estimating the heading of the *Royal Oak*, but an almost equally great mistake in estimating the heading of Prien's own boat, when he had a good navigator and a visual check as well.

Prien gets the *Royal Oak's* position nearly right, but her heading totally and absurdly wrong; it may be significant that her position would have been known with some certainty in Germany, from air reconnaissance, but her precise heading during the hours of darkness could not be known. And there is again the further significant point that the *Repulse*, which must have been photographed at the same time as the *Royal Oak*, is shown in Prien's reports as occupying the position which she did actually occupy – at the time of the air reconnaissance, but not at the time of the sinking.

Equally baffling is Prien's description of the behaviour of the tide. It was coming in at 11.30 p.m. ('following tide'); then, two hours later, at 1.30 a.m., 'it is now low tide'; and a few minutes after that the tide is coming in again at the truly extraordinary speed (even for the Pentland Firth) of ten knots, when it should have been going out. The next high water was not due until 10.20 a.m. The behaviour of tides is, of course, much affected by wind speed and direction, but on that night there was not much wind, either to hold it up or push it on – the log entry shows NNE 3-4, which agrees almost exactly with Skipper Gatt's estimate of NE, light to moderate.

And then again, to enter with a 'following tide' is regarded with astonishment by men who knew those waters far better than Prien could ever have done; quite apart from the fact that it is a recognised thing to negotiate a difficult, tortuous channel by 'stemming' the tide. Of course, Prien says that he stemmed the tide on his retirement from the Flow, which fits with commonsense; it does not, however, fit the tide tables, which indicate that at that time the tide was going out, so that once more he would have had a 'following tide.'

The German official records, in so far as they depend on the testimony of Prien, present therefore a number of apparently inexplicable features. Surviving members of the crew of U-47 might be able to help, but the three all-important witnesses – Prien himself, and his two watch-keeping officers – are dead.

The German records, as regards the planning of the operation, are a totally different matter. They rest on the testimony of Admiral Dönitz, and, furthermore, they agree with the facts as we know them – except for one point, which seems strange.

The Dönitz 'War Diary' corroborates what we already know from survivors, that an intensive air and sea watch was being kept on Scapa Flow. As a result, Dönitz decided that entry through the booms at Hoxa, Switha and Hoy was impossible, but noted that there was a penetrable gap in Kirk Sound which was 170 metres wide and 7 metres deep – information not likely to be obtained by air reconnaissance alone, although this does not necessarily postulate a fulltime resident agent in Orkney. He notes additionally that the principal obstacle to a successful penetration is the actual navigation of Kirk Sound and bases his 'key' times on slack water.

Clearly, he intended the U-boat to approach at slack water, wait for the tide to turn, and then 'stem' through the channel against the tide – both on entering and on leaving. That makes sense – but it does not agree with what Prien says he did. The log of U-47 flouts logic, the tide tables, and the plans of the Commodore, Submarines.

Dönitz records that he laid on a special air reconnaissance for 12th October which showed that, at three o'clock in the afternoon, there were in the anchorage an aircraft carrier, five heavy ships, and ten cruisers. Possibly the *Iron Duke*, *Voltaire* and *Pegasus* were somehow included as something more potent than they really were. The puzzling point is that the pilot of the aircraft was brought to Wilhelmshaven the same night, in order to explain the photographs, and that the news was radioed to U-47, but was not received because she was 'grounded.'

Presumably the message was sent with reasonable despatch, the same night. If so, it is curious that Prien did not receive it because, according to his log, he 'surfaced in the evening and came in to the coast in order to fix exact position of ship.' It is stranger still that he did not receive it next day or on the following night. There was plenty of time – all day and half the night of Friday, 13th October. Submarines then normally came up at night – indeed, they had to – but even for submarines 'grounded' during daylight there was nevertheless a perfectly normal routine for the reception of messages; and this routine took into account that the submarine might miss one or more transmissions of the message. This was a particularly important message regarding a particularly important operation; and must also have been expected. But it was not received.

Yet, judging by Prien's log, it was received. For how else could he have got the information, accurate – but slightly out of date – that the *Repulse* was lying next to the *Royal Oak*. The *Repulse* was not there for long; she had only just returned to Scapa from the abortive chase in the gale after the *Gneisnau* and *Köln*, and she put to sea again shortly afterwards. He claimed to have hit a ship which was not there, but had been there, in that position, not long before. It is hardly likely that, out of the entile Home Fleet, he should pick on that particular ship for his false claim, unless he had reason to believe she would be where he thought he saw her. That is, presuming that he himself was there, and that the whole U-boat story is not a fake from beginning to end.

Taken together then, the German official documents present a baffling mass of contradictions, hard to resolve. It is difficult to avoid the conclusion that some vital part of the story is 'missing from the record.'

From the British side, too, there are some features which are truly remarkable – assuming, that is, that the *Royal Oak* was sunk by torpedo. The first is that the ship was stored a few hours before the explosions occurred, and that the explosions took place in, or in the vicinity of, storerooms where stores had just been loaded. And nowhere else. Even if we accept that a torpedo salvo striking amidships – on the starboard side only – would automatically involve the central stores, there is still that first explosion right forward in the bows, which actually flooded the inflammable store. If it is a coincidence, it is certainly a very strange one.

But once again we have to make allowances, not merely for a single coincidence, but for many. We know that the target was vast, stationary, and virtually unmissable from the range at which a U-boat must have fired. Therefore we have to believe that all three torpedoes of the first salvo, as well as the torpedo fired afterwards from the stern, were mechanically defective, the only one to score a hit striking a storeroom in the bows. We have to believe that all the torpedoes of the second salvo ran perfectly and that, by accident, each one also struck a storeroom. And we are unable to account for the three missing torpedoes, of which no trace was ever found.

It is also necessary to explain – in some cases, virtually to explain away – the observed results of explosions which would appear, theoretically, not to be from a torpedo. We are again faced with a succession of coincidences.

The first explosion appeared to raise no column of spray, although it occurred in comparatively shallow water; certainly Leading Signalman Fossey, looking forward from the flag-deck, did not see it. Because the cables ran out, he assumed that it had occurred on the centreline of the ship, not at the side. The bows were narrow, and unprotected by 'blisters,' and therefore that is not conclusive; but it was the inflammable store which flooded – and it was there that stores had been put the previous day.

The second explosion, which was much more violent, virtually wiped out all the witnesses; it proved impossible to contact anyone who was in the Boys' messdeck at the time, so few of them survived.

The third explosion was more violent still and occurred deep inside the ship, at the approximate location of the Central Stores, which were on the starboard side, but inboard. If it was a torpedo, then it had penetrated the starboard 'blisters' at their widest point, approximately amidships, penetrated or blown open several more cornpartments, blown upwards from somewhere near the bottom of the hull clean through the armoured deck and sent both blast and flash as high up as the CPOs' and POs' Recreation Space in the superstructure above the *port* battery. It struck there with sufficient force to splinter the furniture and burn Supply Petty Officer Finley so badly that he was in hospital for six weeks. But even more extraordinary is that it blew open the armoured deck, two decks below, which was designed to keep out heavy shells falling almost vertically on the ship at enormous speeds. And the flash not only travelled up, but sideways from the cross-passage on the centre-line, cutting down most of the stokers.

The fourth explosion, curiously enough, did not penetrate to anything like the same extent, but it certainly blew upwards to a remarkable degree, for the starboard side of the Marines' messdeck collapsed. And in this case, too, it coincided with the scores which here were actually on the starboard side, not inboard as they were amidships. It is even more curious, when we consider that at this point the 'blisters' begin to taper off.

There appears to have been a quite remarkable variation in the effect of the explosions, assuming that they were caused by torpedoes. The first explosion was a very minor affair; the second we know little of, except that it did not touch the Communications mess on the port side opposite; the third torpedo, if it was a torpedo, penetrated enormously; the fourth not nearly so much. Even allowing for the known capriciousness of explosives, this is strange; it could be readily explained by two alternatives only: that the explosions were in fact internal, and came from the storerooms, variously located, or that two different types of torpedo were used, the third explosion being caused by a 'fish' which was moving very much faster than the others.

Theoretically, this is possible. But we know that, in fact, it was not so. All the torpedoes used, according to Dönitz, were of the comparatively slow 'trackless' type powered by electric motors. The normal type of torpedo, which leaves a tell-tale trail of bubbles, but is very much faster, was not used. It is not possible even to speculate on the effects of torpedoes fitted with magnetic 'pistols' which would explode underneath the ship; the log of U-47 specifically states that 'impact fuses' were fitted, and, as the target was a big ship in comparatively shallow water, this is almost certainly true.

It is noteworthy that the survivors who believed most strongly in sabotage contained a high proportion of those who had been in the unfortunate position of knowing with fair precision where some of the explosions were and what were their results; in particular, those who were put in hospital by the flash from the third explosion. On the other hand, some of the men convinced – not at the time, but after the official announcement – that the explosions were caused by torpedoes, had not had those opportunities; in particular, a number who had been caught by the cordite flame near the night 'heads,' and also the officers aft on the quarter-deck. None of the officers interviewed believed any longer in sabotage, but almost two-thirds of the ratings did.

Often enough the latter, after being interviewed and having come uninterrupted to the end of their personal stories, would stop, pause, and then say, flatly: 'Well, it wasn't torpedo, I tell you that straight.' Others again would seem embarrassed for a moment before asking, casually, 'Have you come across anything... odd... about the *Royal Oak?*'

•   •   •

Rarely can there have been such doubt, by eye-witnesses, of an accepted and officially confirmed story. There were, in fact, too many contradictions, too many coincidences, and too many inexplicable happenings, even without the additional proof of the faking of Prien's log. Evidence for torpedo was all very well, but throughout the enquiry, it merely marched step by step with equally convincing evidence for sabotage.

There was no parallel even with the similar cases of the *Vanguard*, *Natal* and *Bulwark*, where the causes of the explosions had been problematical. Here, a comparatively large number of men had survived and could testify. To find an equivalent mystery one would have to go back as far as the days of sail, when the *Royal George*, anchored at Spithead, in the middle of the fleet, simply fell over on her side and vanished in about fifteen seconds, a proceeding inadequately explained by the pious belief that a gust of wind had upset her.

One could prove, laboriously, that this was technical nonsense and that anyway the wind was from the bow, not the beam, and that the additional theory, that she was over-heeled by her captain, was equally untenable. But it is, in this case, unnecessary. Those concerned being dead and the need for secrecy long since passed away, the true story may be found in the Minutes of the Court-Martial, now in the Public Record Office. What is interesting, however, was that those Minutes were suppressed at the time – although there was one 'leak' to a newspaper – and that a contractor who tried to raise the wreck met continual obstruction from the local authorities and was subsequently ruined. The one thing that authority did not want to see again was the *Royal George* – because they knew perfectly well that the only explanation which fitted all the facts and the testimony of 'key' witnesses was that the bottom had fallen out of her.

To preserve a secret so disturbing they were prepared to see the contractor ruined and the Captain traduced by untrue accusations that he had over-heeled his ship. They did not themselves spread the stories, but, knowing the truth, allowed them to go uncontradicted and, eventually, to achieve immortality in a poem by Cowper which almost every schoolboy learns.

The poem had also the virtue of being both a simple and a highly dramatic explanation of the disaster, which is partly why it has endured. It cannot be doubted that the stories of Prien and the 'Watchmaker of Kirkwall,' which possess the same qualities to a marked degree, will equally endure.

•   •   •

At the time of the last Survey, in 1951, the *Royal Oak* lay on her starboard side at an angle of 110° from the vertical, slowly sinking into the sandy bottom and turning over, with her 15-inch guns forced up to full elevation and the masts and funnel buckling upwards. All along her port side, which had a least depth of thirty feet of water over it, seaweed was growing in profusion; wherever faint light could penetrate down from the surface to her upper decks and keel there were marine growths of shell and anemone. The bows were clear of the sand and divers could walk under the forepart of the ship for a distance of some fifty or sixty feet. The stern and keel were blown away in the paint store area, and amidships, where the engine rooms, boiler rooms and central stores were located, was a chaos of wreckage blurred by the silt which arose from the divers' movements. The purpose of this Survey was to salvage the propellers, which were valuable metal, and to obtain one anchor. When the anchor cable was found and raised, it came up with unexpected ease, which was explained when it was seen that there was no anchor on the other end. At first sight, this seemed to confirm the theory held by some of the surviving officers, that the first torpedo had actually struck the anchor cable, not the ship itself; but, on examination, the cable appeared to have been severed by an oxy arc cutter.

In December, 1957, the Admiralty invited tenders for the salvage and scrapping of the wreck, but this brought a storm of protest from relatives who felt that the hull of the *Royal Oak* was in a sense the tomb of 800 men and that to disturb it would be desecration. Letters were written to 'The *Evening News*,' Portsmouth – the home port of the ship – from as far afield as Aberdeen; and when reporters went out to interview relatives of the dead men, they found that there existed the strongest opposition to the scheme. 'You would not go to a cemetery and dig up coffins,' said one. 'These sailors have no proper graves,' said another, 'they should be left in peace where they are.' In fact of these protests the Admiralty had to abandon the project; and now, in peace they lie.

APPENDIX

Acknowledgements

I must express my gratitude to the many people who gave freely of their time in order to help me reconstruct the events as precisely as possible. Thirty-three witnesses were interviewed at length; many others wrote for me long and detailed accounts. Others again went to great trouble to help track down 'key' witnesses among the survivors.

For the contemporary narratives, which were especially valuable, I am deeply indebted to Mr J Kerr, who loaned me his scrapbook which contained not only his own very full account but the stories of twelve other survivors who were with him at the time in hospital; to the Headmaster of Ardvreck, for permission to quote from Midshipman Pirie's narrative, which was published in the December, 1939, issue of the school magazine; to Skipper Gatt for unearthing after much search a Toc H pamphlet, 'Sea Samaritans,' containing a reprint from 'The Orcadian' of 10th October, 1940, of his article on the rescue operations; and to Mr R Jones for letting me see a copy of 'The Citizen,' of 30th October, 1939, in which his own personal experiences were reported at length. A number of survivors were able to supply photographs, most of which had in fact been taken by SBA Bendell, who does not have a complete set, because his negatives are still in the wreck.

It was intended to contact at least ten per cent of the survivors in order to achieve a reasonable cross-section of the ship's company; this was more than achieved, but there are nevertheless a few gaps, due to heavy casualties in particular messes. I have not attempted to fill these by hearsay because, although most of those stories which were related at second proved on further investigation to be basically true, there had been a certain blurring of detail; they had deteriorated with age, whereas first-hand experiences had been too vivid to forget.

I have to thank the following survivors of HMS *Royal Oak* for their help in The reconstruction:

	Rank at the Time
Commander G Affleck-Graves, RN(Retd.)	Flag Lieutenant
Mr W G T Batterbury	Leading Supply Assistant
SBCPO R G Bendell, RN	Sick Berth Attendant
Major M H Benton, RM (Retd.)	Lieutenant, RM
Lieutenant T W Blundell, RN (Retd.)	A/Petty Officer
Mr G H Booth	Sergeant, RM
Surgeon Captain E D Caldwell, RN	Surgeon Lieutenant
Mr H P Cleverley	Stoker
Rear-Admiral (S) J R Cundall, CBE, RN (Retd.)	Paymaster Commander
Mr E G Donunett	Ordnance Artificer
Commander H Duncan. DSC, RN	Lieutenant
Mr A J Farley	Able Seaman
Mr N J Finley	Supply Petty Officer
Mr W J Fossey	Leading Signalman
Mr B S C Hawes	Marine
Lieutenant H J Instance, RN	Leading Seaman
Mr T H Jones	Leading Stoker
Mr R S Jones	Leading Telegraphist
Major B Keen, RM (Retd.)	Lieutenant, RM
Mr J R Kerr	Petty Officer (Div. PO)
Mr A Lawrence, DSM and Bar	Chief Stoker
Mr J McLaverty	Sergeant, R.M.
Captain R F Nichols, RN (Retd.)	Commander
Mr P H Owen	Cadet
Mr W Owens	Marine
Mr G E T Parham	Sergeant, RM
Lieutenant R P Pirie, RN (Retd.)	Midshipman Engineer
Commander J W Renshaw, OBE, RN, (Retd.)	Engineer

Commander Mr S R Saltmarsh	Marine
Commander G E L Sclater, DSO, RN (Retd.)	Lieutenant
Lieutenant E W Scovell, RN	Boy Stores
CPO F G Sims, RN	Leading Supply Assistant
Mr G L Trewinnard	Boy
Mr C G Wilson	Chief ERA.

and, of course. Skipper J G Gatt, DSC, master of the *Daisy II*. While in hospital, Mr Kerr wrote down the stories of the following additional survivors: Chief Stoker P Terry, Marine Moore, Stoker W M Campbell, Stoker A Bond, Stoker O L Fletcher, Musician J F P Thompson, Able Seaman W Hancock, and Ordinary Seaman J V Hearn; I have drawn upon these.

I have also to thank Capcain W R Fell, RN (Retd.) and Mr J L McKay, naval diver, for their recollections of the 1951 Survey; Mr E Wheeler, for his account of what happened in the Admiralty water carrier *Fountain* at Lyness; Mr D H Allan, formerly a Police Constable at Kirkwall, for his recollections and much help besides in obtaining from Merchant Navy sources authoritative opinions on Kirk Sound; to Mrs B Gunn, of 2, Duncan Street, Thurso, for her memories of that 'dark winter's night' when the survivors were brought to her door; and to Mr E W Marwick, Editor of 'The Orkney Herald,' for letting me have the results of his researches into the stories of 'The Watchmaker of Kirkwall' as well as generously allowing me space in which to contact local witnesses. I have also to thank, for their help in contacting survivors, the Editor of 'The Evening News,' Portsmouth, the Editor of 'The Sunderland Echo & Shipping Gazette,' and the Editor of 'The Evening Express,' Aberdeen.

In conclusion, I must express my gratitude to a number of relatives of those who lost their lives in HMS *Royal Oak*, for help which they were able to give me in various ways; I must mention in particular Mrs Constance Avery, of Southsea, who lost a brother, Mrs Audrey Osborne, of Portsmouth, who lost her father, and Mr T Jackson, of Houghton-le-Spring, Co. Durham, who lost his son. I hope that this book will in some measure, be a memorial to them and their comrades.